Dealing with your Demons

Exercising Faith Through Spiritual Warfare

Santosh Kumar

INDIA • SINGAPORE • MALAYSIA

ISBN

Hardcase 979-8-89475-468-0
Paperback 979-8-89475-467-3

Dedication

To the source of my life and my existence,

My God!

Contents

Acknowledgement

First and foremost, I dedicate this book to God Almighty. Without His boundless grace, unwavering love, and divine guidance, this work would not have been possible. All glory and honor belong to Him, the source of all wisdom and strength.

To my beloved family, especially my dear wife Rinpuii, your steadfast support and unending encouragement have been my bedrock. Thank you for your patience, love, and understanding throughout this journey. You have been my inspiration and my motivation in every step. To my dear parents, thank you for this life. I am forever grateful to you both.

To my dear friends, your companionship and prayers have been a vital part of this process. Thank you for standing by me, offering words of wisdom and comfort, and always believing in this vision.

Finally, to all my fellow Christians who are engaged in spiritual warfare, this book is for you. Your courage, faith, and perseverance in the face of adversity are a testament to the power of God's love and the strength found in Christ. May this book serve as a source of encouragement and a reminder that you are never alone in this fight. Together, we stand strong in the Lord and in His mighty power.

Thank you all for your support and belief in this mission. May God bless each and every one of you abundantly.

Preface

Sin, disobedience, and immorality are engraved in humans, an evident characteristic of their vulnerability and need for redemption. The devil's involvement in God's most treasured possession (human) is to destroy and isolate them from their creator. The active or passive complicity of the devil and his agents in human life has resulted in misery, devastation, and destruction. Anti-creation concepts comprised the functionality of this world, rejecting or perhaps ignoring the divine concept of creation. Demonic oppression has almost gripped the community today, where no one is safe, happy, or prosperous. The basic needs of society are compromised by devilish agendas, which are not prosperous but the ultimate destruction of human civilization. The Devil's handiwork encompasses all the malevolent elements he has introduced into the world, aimed at undermining God's creations, including conflicts, illnesses, diseases, intellectual missteps, temptations to sin, pornography, easy divorce, false prophecy, heresy, and the like.

Contemporary Christian societies can often be seen as muzzling on the issues of demonization, deliverance ministry, and spiritual issues. The church shies away from the subject, claiming that talking about the devil is equal to glorifying him (Richard Ing 1996, 7). Charles H. Kraft, speaking in the Nigerian Christian context, states that modern-day Christianity is viewed as a love-filled, transforming faith, most likely similar to New Testament Christianity. However, it lacks the power of the New Testament. Today, Christianity lacks the ability to deal with spiritual issues. He further stated that this ignorance has been adapted from Western missionaries (Kraft 2017, xii).

God, in His infinite wisdom, intended humankind to flourish and not destroy. The redemptive demonstration of God for humankind can be seen in the Cross of Calvary. Proof of His interest in intervening in the scene of "paradise lost" towards "paradise regained." The great battle between Christ and the devil is proof of God's redemptive interest towards devil's destructive intention. Recognizing and combating the devil is essential for Christians. Equipping themselves with knowledge of spiritual warfare will enable them to effectively fight against demonic forces and maintain their faith. Of course, with the power of the Holy Spirit and the guidance of God's word—the Bible.

This book attempts to identify, target, and respond to the devil's filthy means and his ferocious attempts to destroy us physically and spiritually. Step by step, the book exposes the devil, reveals his identity, and presents believers to be equipped with spiritual weapons and strategies to defeat the greatest enemy of humankind.

Santosh Kumar, DMiss

Chapter 1

The Cosmic Conflict

> *"For you have said in your heart: 'I will ascend into heaven, I will exalt my throne above the stars of God; I will also sit on the mount of the congregation. On the farthest sides of the north; I will ascend above the heights of the clouds, I will be like the Most High.'"*
> ***Isaiah 14:13,14***

God is love (1 Jn 4:16), the most significant and concrete characteristic of God, which is established as the foundation of faith. God created the earth, extending his expounding mercy which must "endure forever" (Ps. 107:1). In His abundant mercy and love, God presented the freedom of choice to humankind. Heaven was privileged in ancient times, prior to the creation of the earth and the downfall of humanity. All God's creations exercised the gift of choice. Unfortunately, *hêylêl* or "Lucifer, the morning star" (Isa. 14:12), guardian cherub (Eze. 28:14) had a conflict of interest with God and questioned his supremacy due to pride and a desire for power, rebelled against God. The notion of free will is an essential tenet in Christianity. God has bestowed upon beings, including angels, the ability to make choices, whether good or bad. In this regard, Lucifer's rebellion can be perceived as a misuse of this divine gift. Rather than choosing to align with God's will, Lucifer opted to rebel, which resulted in his condemnation.

The disagreement between God and Lucifer is rooted in the latter's pride and aspiration for independence. Lucifer sought to emulate God or even surpass Him, leading to a fundamental clash of interests. In this theological framework, God, as the supreme and benevolent being, could not tolerate any form of rebellion against His divine order. The gift of choice that God had given mankind was disregarded and disrupted by Lucifer's influence, leading to a violation of God's will.

Conflict of Interest has always been a common issue in society worldwide. Every conscious and subconscious mind clearly understands and distinguishes good from evil. It is perhaps, or indeed, the choice a person makes, either to opt for good or evil. Conflicts of interest are not confined to humans. Lucifer, in his innermost being, commenced to exalt himself, thereby perverting the intent of his creation as any other created angel, which was to safeguard the righteous (Ps 91:11, 12), dwell in heaven (Matt 28:2; Jn 1:51), serve as God's warrior (Matt 26:53), worship God (Lk 2:13), and extol God's glory (Lk 2:13-14; Isa 6:2-4). Rather than obeying, acknowledging, and appreciating the awe-inspiring works of the Almighty, this creature chose to revolt, leading to the disruptive and catastrophic separation between the Creator and His creation.

As previously mentioned, the gift of free will is conferred with the intention of aligning oneself with the divine plan of God. God's creations are granted the ability to make choices, and their decisions are not predetermined by God. Lucifer's rebellion is seen because of his own misuse of the free will that God granted him.

The gist of the cosmic conflict lies in Lucifer's rebellion, as it represents the ultimate struggle between the realms of good and evil. Lucifer, a formerly exalted and potent celestial being, engaged in the act of defiance against God's divine authority by challenging his supremacy. The uprising resulted in a universal confrontation that affected all individuals inhabiting the Earth. The narrative of Lucifer's rebellion functions as a cautionary anecdote regarding the dangers of conceitedness, self-centeredness, and pursuit of authority. Additionally, it highlights the significance of our action and the consequences of our decisions. The cosmic conflict between morality and immorality prompts us to inhabit a realm where we are perpetually faced with the decision to opt for good or evil and that our decisions carry tangible and enduring consequences. The story of Lucifer's rebellion serves as a potent admonition of the significance of adhering to our principles based on God's word and convictions despite encountering hardship and temptations.

We will be discussing cosmic conflict, the most important battle affecting every human being on this earth. This chapter examines and delineates major controversies and opponents before addressing them.

The Great Controversy

The theme of Great Controversy holds a significant position in the Bible and is evident in numerous scriptural teachings. The Great Controversy is a theological notion that pertains to the universal struggle between righteousness and wickedness, as depicted in the Bible. This conflict is illustrated through the narrative of Lucifer's rebellion against the divine being, serving as a potent reminder of the significance of autonomous agency and the repercussions of our decisions.

The act of rebellion by created beings against their creator resulted in the loss of their identity, magnificence, and even existence. The cosmic conflict resulted in Lucifer's transformation into the devil who directed accusations against the Holy of Holies, deceiving others regarding the divine character of God, which in actual is rooted in love. One-third of the angels were deceived by a false paradox that led to their separation from God and heaven. According to Ellen G. White, God demonstrated immense mercy by tolerating Lucifer's malevolent actions for an extended period. According to White (1999), discontentment and disaffection in heaven were unfamiliar and novel. It was crucial to eliminate this novel and threatening sensation from the heavenly realm. Nevertheless, God opted to spare him in his never-ending compassion instead of annihilating him. The benevolence of God's grace towards the rebel, Satan and his associates, indicates God's loving nature and His lack of intention to enforce His ideas, strategies, and judgments upon His created beings.

Notwithstanding this, inquiries may emerge as to why God chose not to eliminate sin immediately, thereby leading the future of peace for humanity.

What is the reason for the continued existence of evil forces in the realm of God's creation? What are the reasons for experiencing suffering? Given God's omniscience and omnipotence, it is reasonable to question why His creation must endure the affliction of the sin's curse. What is God's inability to completely eradicate the presence of sin, the devil, and his cohorts? According to John C. Peckham (2018), the evil attributed to the devil is momentary in nature, and any hasty attempt to eliminate it may lead to irreparable harm to the good. (p. 56). According to Grant R. Osborne, as cited in Peckham, the conflict in the cosmos is irreversible and non-negotiable. The dichotomy between good and evil is inevitable and leaves no room for neutrality. According to Peckham (2010), individuals are affiliated with either the dominion of God or the dominion of evil, and these two entities coexist in the world.

The narrative of Lucifer's rebellion towards the divine is an instructive anecdote that underscores the threats of pride and the importance of cultivating humility. The early church placed great importance on the cross, symbolizing the need to remain steadfast in one's values and beliefs, despite encountering challenges and enticements (Ferguson 2009, 596).

Who is Guilty?

As discussed above, God cannot and must not be blamed for what was caused by a selfish culprit. God's grace is extraordinary enough to engulf the devil's mischievousness. In her book Patriarchs and Prophets (1890), Ellen G. White says,

> Lucifer is convinced that he is wrong. He saw that "the Lord is righteous in all His ways, and holy in all His works" (Psalm 145:17); that the divine statutes are just, and that he ought to acknowledge them as such before all heaven. Had he done this, he might have saved himself and many angels. He had not at that time fully cast off his allegiance to God. Though he had left his position as covering cherub, yet if he had been willing to return to God, acknowledging the Creator's wisdom, and satisfied to fill

> the place appointed him in God's great plan, he would have been reinstated in his office. 39

Lucifer's decline from his exalted position was attributed to his reluctance to exhibit humility and his desire for authority and dominance in heaven, above God. Lucifer, a divine creation of God, chose to rebel against the Kingdom of God because of his erroneous thoughts, which led to his expulsion from heaven. Presently, the devil persists in employing his traditional tactics, persistently devising, and scheming to sabotage the divine blueprint for humankind, "be fruitful and multiply; fill the earth and subdue it... (Gen 1:28). However, the devil is proactively engaged with this world to cause separation between God and us.

Therefore, it is imperative for us, especially those who holds Christian beliefs to possess knowledge regarding the strategies employed by the devil and to maintain a state of alertness to counteract their conspiracies. It is crucial to cultivate a sense of humility, exhibit self-control in the face of temptation, and remain steady in upholding core values and beliefs. Lucifer's rebellion serves as a poignant indication that our decisions carry tangible and enduring outcomes and that we must exercise prudence in our choices if we aspire to surmount the malevolent influences and lead a life imbued with significance.

Even though Lucifer is responsible for this chaos, it's important to recognize that the cosmic battle is both real and continuous. We must be knowledgeable of its impact and significance on our lives.

The Great Controversy Continues

Although the Bible opens with a description of unformed earth in Genesis 1, it was unaffected by sin or evil. "The earth was without form, and void; and darkness was on the face of the deep. The Spirit of God was hovering over the face of the waters" (Gen. 1:2). In Gen. 1:3-27, we can read how magnificently God garnishes the earth and everything around it (Gen. 1:3-27).

The Bible mentions, "The Lord God planted a garden eastward in Eden, and there He put the man whom He had formed" (Gen. 2:8). The Lord established everything in the Garden of Eden and placed man to care for and manage it (Gen. 2:15). Not only did God establish man as the keeper of the garden, he also made him a companion, Eve, who would be with him so that the man would not be alone (Gen. 2:18).

However, this celebration was momentary. Life in God's Garden was joyous until the devil was impersonated as a serpent (personification of evil), to make the greatest annihilation by destroying the blissful relationship between God and Humankind. The serpent persuades Eve to take an interest in the fruits of the forbidden tree that God commanded not to eat. The serpent says, "...Has God indeed said, 'You shall not eat of every tress of the garden'?" (Gen. 3:1). In retort, Eve corrects the serpent (Gen.3:2-3), "We may eat the fruit of the trees of the garden; but of the fruit of the tree which is in the midst of the garden, God has said, 'You shall not eat it, nor shall you touch it, lest you die.' "The serpent for the first time directly rebuttals Eve's notion about the forbidden trees. He says, "...You will not surely die" (Gen. 3:4a). This was the first time that the devil revealed his opinions regarding God. In the continuous dialogue with the woman, the serpent continues, "For God knows that in the day you eat of it, your eyes will be opened, and you will be like God, knowing good and evil' (Gen. 3:5).

The devil's persuasion of inculcating disbelief about God in Eve's heart was futile until Eve's eye beheld the forbidden tree. "So when the woman saw that the tree was good for food, that it was pleasant to the eyes, and a tree desirable to make one wise, she took of its fruit and ate..." (Gen. 3:6). Although a significant part of human disobedience had to blame the devil, it is undeniable that Eve was influenced by the desire to obtain the fruits of the forbidden tree. Eve became the instrument in creating a huge chasm between the Divine being and humankind. Adam also participated in the delinquency.

The first couple declared their separation from God and allegiance to the devil after choosing to listen to the devil's conspiratorial claims. This action had spiritually and intentionally alienated them from God. In the cool of the day, when God walks into the garden, the sense of alienation is unambiguous. "And they heard the sound of the Lord God walking in the garden in the cool of the day, and Adam and his wife hid themselves from the presence of the Lord God among the trees of the garden" (Gen. 3:9).

Jacques Doukhan (2016) mentions,

> Adam and Eve shift from the immediate world of seeing and touching, which is associated with the deception of the serpent, to the world of hearing, which implies the distance of the divine presence (Deut. 6:4). While the serpent has come closer, God has seemingly become distant. 94

Apparently, there is no longer cherishing moment when Adam and Eve would share with their creators. The divine-human rendezvous is obviously desecrated.

The concept of conflict between good and evil forces has been prevalent since the dawn of humanity. The ongoing conflict between entities representing good and evil persists even to the present time.

Religions worldwide teach various aspects, including moral values, the concepts of good and evil. However, many religious narratives have lost the actual story and the culprit over time. The Bible, on the other hand, consistently reminds us of these crucial elements throughout. These aspects not only serve as reminders but also inspire believers to maintain their faith in God. In the ongoing great controversy, God seeks our allegiance. Like the trust placed in humans in the Garden of Eden, where God granted authority over everything, God expressed His love to win human hearts. The divine desire is for humanity to reconcile with God, restoring the broken relationship by aligning with Him and standing against the devil in the cosmic battle.

To achieve this, God freely offers salvation to all people, irrespective of their race or the time they live in. All that humanity needs to do is remain loyal to God, worship Him exclusively, and glorify Him amidst the cosmic conflict.

Theologians encountered a shared predicament regarding the means of attaining salvation, which influenced their answers in accordance with a common theological framework. Most emphasized the significance of performing righteous deeds or virtuous actions while advocating for reliance on a higher power for deliverance (Dass 2018, 45). The concept of salvation by faith alone originated in the Bible, specifically in the New Testament. In his epistle addressed to the Ephesians, Paul articulated the notion that salvation is a result of divine grace and faith rather than personal effort or merit. He asserts that this salvation is not a product of human agency but rather a gift bestowed by God, and thus cannot be attributed to any individual's accomplishments or achievements. This concept is conveyed in the following passage: "For it is by grace you have been saved, through faith—and this is not from yourselves, it is the gift of God—not by works, so that no one can boast" (Ephesians 2:8-9). This passage highlights the belief that salvation is a divine endowment acquired through faith rather than good deeds or accomplishments.

The significance of the doctrine of salvation by faith alone in Christianity lies in its emphasis on the pivotal role of faith in Jesus Christ as the sole means to attain salvation. Salvation is contingent upon an individual's faith in Jesus Christ as their Lord and Savior, rather than their ethical conduct or virtuous disposition. This conviction entails more than a mere cognitive acknowledgment of Jesus' existence; rather, it involves profound and intimate reliance on Him as the exclusive means to attain an everlasting life. Placing absolute trust in Jesus becomes achievable only when we can uncover the decisive role of the devil in this world. This understanding is attainable when we learn how to identify the devil, recognizing it as our adversary.

Identifying the Enemy

Lucifer, also referred to as Satan or the devil, is recognized as an adversary in spiritual warfare. It is imperative to recognize his schemes and sway to defeat him effectively. Lucifer is frequently linked to pride and arrogance because of his conviction that he can match or surpass the power of God. The individual's sense of self-importance instigated a rebelliousness of divine authority and yearning for deification. The employment of arrogance is a prevalent strategy utilized by adversaries, intending to delude individuals into believing that they possess the ability to emulate the divine and act according to their own desires. Lucifer is commonly recognized as a progenitor of falsehoods and trickery. Lucifer's mission is to cause harm and create divisions. The serpent perpetrated deception upon Eve in the Garden of Eden, and its deceptive tactics persist today. Detecting dishonest statements from an individual can be tricky because they often have a subtle quality. This emphasizes the importance of staying vigilant and paying close attention to what they say. Understanding whether God's teachings are true or not requires being good in identifying what is true and what is not.

The significance of striving for harmony and tranquility and advocating ethical and virtuous conduct cannot be overstated. Lucifer was commonly linked to obscurity and evil. He personifies malevolence and stands in opposition to all that are virtuous and just. It is imperative to possess spiritual readiness and proficiency to combat adversaries. This necessitates a robust belief in the divine being firmly rooted in the veracity of the divine scripture and imbued with the Holy Ghost. This conflict with Lucifer transcends individual concerns and has global implications. His influence is evident in various domains including religious and political conflicts, environmental concerns, social inequality, and ethical degradation.

By acknowledging their impact in these domains, individuals can strive towards advancing peace, equity, and morality. Ultimately, recognizing Lucifer as a formidable adversary is crucial to engaging in spiritual combat. By identifying and comprehending an individual's strategies and impacts, one can strive to advance virtuous and ethical ideals while simultaneously surmounting malevolent forces. A comprehensive comprehension of spiritual warfare, steadfast dedication to advancing peace and equity, and spiritual readiness to combat the adversary are essential for this endeavor.

Lucifer ruptured his relationship with God to the extent that, in his heart, he knew, there was no turning back. Once full of wisdom and grace, the "guardian cherub," "Lucifer" (star of the morning) became proud of himself and was cast out of heaven. Ellen White (1890) states, "It was too great a sacrifice for one who had been so highly honored to confess that he had been in error, that his imaginings were false, and to yield to the authority which he had been working to prove unjust" (39).

At that moment, Lucifer became an adversary of God. "it was that Lucifer, "the light bearer," the sharer of God's glory, the attendant of His throne, by transgression became Satan, "the adversary" of God and holy beings and the destroyer of those whom Heaven had committed to his guidance and guardianship" (White, 39).

The identification of a spiritual adversary is important for various reasons. Spiritual powers are antagonistic to God. Comprehending the essence of spiritual adversaries can provide ethical and moral directions for individuals and communities. Furthermore, it has the potential to foster introspection and to facilitate individual development.

Recognizing spiritual adversaries and their strategies against God's people is crucial for participating in spiritual warfare and safeguarding oneself from its impact. It is imperative for both individuals and communities to comprehend the essence of spiritual adversaries and their strategies to safeguard themselves and achieve their objectives. Comprehending the essence of spiritual adversaries can provide ethical and moral direction for individuals and societies.

Biblical teachings also emphasize the importance of being cognizant of adversaries and discerning their identities. The biblical text found in Proverbs 27:12 suggests that individuals who possess prudence are able to identify potential hazards and seek shelter, while those who lack this quality continue on their path and suffer consequences. This verse advocates the cultivation of wisdom and the ability to discern potential threats in advance to prevent their escalation into problems.

Additionally, biblical scripture instructs individuals to exhibit love towards their adversaries and offers supplication for those who subject them to mistreatment (Matt 5:44). This proposition suggests that, instead of disregarding or accommodating malevolent actions, we ought to react to adversaries with benevolence and empathy. Through this approach, it is possible to surmount malevolence with benevolence and effectuate constructive transformations on a global scale.

In a nutshell, the Bible instructs us on the significance of recognizing adversaries and reacting to them with benevolence and empathy. It is prudent to exercise discernment and acknowledge potential hazards while concurrently endeavoring to effectuate constructive transformation in society by responding to adversaries with benevolence.

Understanding Spiritual Warfare

The notion of spiritual warfare pertains to the conflict between the opposing forces of good and evil, namely those aligned with God and Satan, respectively, as well as the dichotomy between the powers of light and darkness. Conflict occurs within the spiritual realm and has tangible ramifications in a corporeal reality. The topic of spiritual warfare is extensively expounded in Christian literature, which underscores the significance of employing the authority bestowed upon us by Jesus to counteract the machinations of the devil. The present discourse examines the notion of spiritual warfare, its significance, and practical implications for everyday existence.

The significance of spiritual warfare lies in its ability to facilitate the acknowledgment of the existence of the spiritual realm and evil entities that inhabit it. Furthermore, it facilitates our comprehension of the jurisdiction bestowed on us by Jesus to withstand the devil and his stratagems. As per

Charles H. Kraft's book, "I Give You Authority: Practicing the Authority Jesus Gave Us," spiritual warfare encompasses utilizing the authority bestowed upon us to withstand the devil and his stratagems. The basis of this authority is rooted in our affiliation with Jesus and our beliefs in his teachings. The significance of engaging in spiritual warfare lies in its ability to equip individuals with the necessary tools to conquer the temptations and adversities encountered in their everyday lives. Maintaining a steadfast focus on God enables individuals to withstand the devil's efforts to divert their attention from their religious beliefs.

Comprehending the concept of spiritual warfare is of paramount importance for individuals who identify as Christians and aspire to lead triumphant lives. Spiritual warfare pertains to the conflict between the opposing forces of good and evil, namely God and Satan, and the opposing factions of light and darkness. Conflict occurs within the metaphysical domain and has tangible ramifications in corporeal reality. The present discourse aims to examine the notion of spiritual warfare and its implications for the lives of individuals who identify as Christians.

The Nature of Spiritual Warfare

Spiritual warfare is an undeniable aspect of the Christian experience that all adherents must confront. The conflict in question transpires within the metaphysical domain and has tangible repercussions on corporeal reality. According to biblical teachings, the struggle that we face is not limited to physical entities but extends to the spiritual entities of malevolence that exist in the celestial realms (Ephesians 6:12). Malevolent spiritual entities are under the leadership of Satan, who is regarded as the supreme adversary of a divine being.

According to 2 Corinthians 10:4, the implements utilized in our battles are not corporeal in nature but rather pertain to the spiritual realm. According to Ephesians 6:13-17, individuals are exhorted to assume the complete armor of God, comprising the belt of truth, breastplate of righteousness, shoes of peace, shield of faith, helmet of salvation, and sword of the Spirit, which is identified as the word of God. The utilization of spiritual weapons is imperative for achieving triumph in the realm of spiritual warfare.

The Power of Prayer

The significance of prayer in various religious and spiritual practices has been widely acknowledged. It is considered a means of communication with a higher power or deity and a way to express gratitude, seek guidance, and offer supplication. The act of prayer has been found to have positive effects on mental and emotional well-being and is associated with increased feelings of peace, calmness, and connectedness. Additionally, prayer has been observed to promote a sense of community and social support among individuals who engage together. Overall, the importance of prayer in various contexts cannot be overstated.

The act of prayer is considered a potent tool in spiritual warfare. Prayer serves as a means of establishing communication with the divine, and beseeching divine intervention and safeguarding. The scriptural text of 1 Thessalonians 5:17 instructs individuals to continuously engage in prayer, while Ephesians 6:18 emphasizes the importance of praying in the Spirit during all circumstances.

Prayer can serve as a means of opposing the machinations of the devil. According to James 4:7, individuals are advised to submit to God. One should strive to resist the influence of the devil, as doing so may result in an eventual departure. Through prayer, individuals demonstrate their submission to God and resistance to the temptations and attacks of the devil.

The Importance of Faith

Faith is a crucial element of the arsenal of spiritual warfare. The biblical passage of Hebrews 11:1 provides a definition of faith as being the unwavering confidence in the realization of hoped-for outcomes and a firm belief in the existence of intangible entities. According to the biblical passage in 1 John 5:4, it is by means of faith that individuals can triumph over the world and malevolent spiritual entities.

Faith serves as a means of accessing God's divine power. According to Jesus, having faith as small as a mustard seed would enable one to command a mountain to move from its place, and it would obey. According to Matthew 17:20, individuals possess the capability to achieve anything without limitations. Possession of faith enables individuals to tap into God's divine power, thereby enabling them to surmount any challenges that may arise in their lives.

The Importance of God's Word

The utilization of the word of God serves as a potent tool in the context of spiritual warfare. The discernment of truth and resistance to falsehood propagated by the devil can be achieved by utilizing God's words. According to the Gospel of Matthew (4:1-11), Jesus employed scriptures to withstand Satan's enticements during his time in the desert.

The scriptural text instructs individuals to engage in the practice of meditating on the word of God, both during the day and at night, as stated in Joshua 1:8. Additionally, Psalm 119:11 emphasizes the importance of internalizing the word God by concealing it within one's heart. Acquiring knowledge of biblical scriptures enables individuals to employ them as a means of withstanding the malevolent assaults of the devil and surmounting any impediments that may arise in their personal lives.

Ultimately, the phenomenon of spiritual warfare is an undeniable aspect of Christian faith that all adherents must confront. The conflict at hand is a dichotomy of morality, pitting the divine against evil and the powers of illumination against obscurity. Christians are exhorted to equip themselves with a complete set of spiritual armor provided by God. This armor comprises the belt of truth, breastplate of righteousness, shoes of peace, shield of faith, helmet of salvation, and sword of the Spirit, which is identified as the word of God. Through prayer, faith, and scriptural teachings, individuals can triumph over worldly challenges and dark spiritual forces.

The inevitability of encountering spiritual attacks is a certainty rather than a possibility. Understanding spiritual warfare is crucial as it enables us to engage in battles. Without this knowledge, we would be unprepared to confront the spiritual challenges. It is incumbent upon us to remain vigilant against the adversary, and engaging in spiritual warfare enables us to fulfill this obligation appropriately. The experience of engaging in a spiritual struggle can lead to self-doubt, a re-evaluation of one's beliefs, and a descent into a state of emotional darkness. The most remarkable facet of spiritual warfare entails being subjected to flames of adversity for refinement. Stagnation precludes both progression and failure. Despite its perceived comfort, this was the least favorable option. The scriptural text provides lucid guidance on the nature of spiritual warfare. The Bible says, "For our struggle is not against flesh and blood, but against the rulers, against the authorities, against the powers of this dark world and against the spiritual forces of evil in the heavenly realm." (Ephesians 6:12, NIV). This battle was also real. "For the flesh sets its desire against the Spirit, and the Spirit against the flesh; for these are in opposition to one another, so that you may not do the things that you please." (Galatians 5:17). Satan's intention is to destroy us by intimidating and isolating us. As a result, God's plan was to deliver us with suffering and proclamation. The Bible says, "Be alert and of sober mind'. Your enemy the devil prowls around like a roaring lion looking for someone to devour." (1 Peter 5:8).

Why was this neglected in the past?

The discourse surrounding spiritual warfare has undergone a notable shift in recent times, with a greater degree of attention and analysis devoted to this topic. Why so? There are numerous factors, both recognized and unrecognized, that have contributed to the historical disregard of this subject. However, I would like to draw attention to a significant factor that has played a role in this neglect.

The term "weltanschauung," originating from German, refers to a comprehensive perspective on the world and human existence, commonly known as a worldview. The origins of the notion of worldview can be attributed to two main sources within the evangelical Protestant community: James Orr, a Scottish Presbyterian theologian who lived between 1844 and 1913, and Abraham Kuyper, a Dutch Neo-Calvinist who lived from 1837 to 1920. Both Orr and Kuyper were influenced by the theological traditions of the reformers from Geneva, particularly John Calvin (1509-64) (Naugle (2002, p.5).

According to Paul G. Hiebert, Worldview can be defined as the fundamental cognitive, affective, and evaluative presumptions and structures that a particular group of individuals forms regarding the essence of reality, which they employ to organize and regulate their daily existence. According to Hiebert (2008), individuals possess a mental representation or cognitive schema of the world they employ to navigate their daily lives. This schema encompasses the perceptions of various phenomena and objects.

According to Charles H. Kraft stated by Apostle Paul that the tactics of the adversary are familiar to us (2 Cor. 2:11). However, contemporary individuals are considerably less inclined to possess the knowledge of the aforementioned individuals. The contemporary populace of Paul's era comprehended the realm of spirits. Owing to the cognitive limitations imposed by our worldviews, we cannot perceive certain aspects of reality. Owing to the lack of knowledge about the adversary during the war, engaging in combat (or evading or retreating) can significantly disadvantage one (Hiebert 2012, 154).

Three fundamental objections

Boyd mentions, "The cultures of the Old and New Testaments, like most ancient and primordial cultures, exemplify a warfare worldview: a fundamental view of the world as engulfed by spiritual beings who are, at least at times, in conflict with one another and whose behavior significantly affects our lives, for better or for worse" (1997, 32). Boyd concluded the following three objectives:

First, the apologetic need for a warfare perspective on suffering and evil will not be seen if there is insufficient appreciation for the radicality of evil in our world, and the radical nature of the problem this poses for the classical philosophical understanding of divine sovereignty as meticulous control. ***Second***, this thesis requires a willingness to think about the power of God, the reality of evil, and Satan's influence in some rather untraditional ways. This point disturbs many more traditionally minded believers. ***Third***, the warfare thesis requires, as a central component, a belief in angels, Satan, and demons as real, autonomous, free agents, as well as a belief that the activity of these beings intersects with human affairs, for better or worse. Many modern people, including Christian theists, find this belief inherently implausible (Boyd, 1997, p.32).

Warfare Worldview

The worldview of warfare is founded on the belief that our universe is involved in a cosmic war between a multitude of agents, both human and angelic, who have chosen to serve either God or Satan. We believe that this worldview best matches the biblical depiction of the response to evil. For example, Jesus categorically condemned calamities such as sickness, demonization, and even natural disasters (i.e., Jesus rebuked the storm) as being the result of Satan's, fallen angels, and sinful people's wills rather than God's.

This viewpoint is not ontologically dualistic because the Bible clearly articulates both the conflict between good and evil, as well as God's sovereignty. The battle that is currently happening will not last forever, and when it does, God's victory will be guaranteed. In fact, victory has already been won through Christ's life, death, and resurrection (Col. 2:13–14), but the defeat of evil has yet to be fully realized. Through prayer, evangelism, and social actions, Christians are called to fight spiritual warfare (Eph. 6:10–17) against evil.

Instead of accepting our circumstances when confronted with evil, the warfare worldview encourages Christians to revolt against evil as evidence of Satan's activity rather than God's mysterious will. Satan, fallen angels, and sinful people have wills of their own, and they are responsible for all that is contrary to God's character, as revealed by Jesus Christ.

Spiritual Warfare in the Old Testament

***The passage of Isaiah 14:12-20*:** The biblical passage of Isaiah 14:12-20 delineates the account of Satan's rebellion against the divine authority. This statement is a potent illustration of the significance of individual agencies and the resultant outcomes stemming from our decisions. Satan's rebellion was not merely an individualistic choice but also impacted a significant portion of the angelic host, as one-third of them chose to align with him. The repercussions of this cosmic rebellion have had enduring effects on humanity, which persist in contemporary times.

Isaiah 14:12-20 says, "How you are fallen from heaven, O Lucifer, son of the morning! How you are cut down to the ground, you who **weakened** the nations! For you have **said in your heart**: 'I will ascend into heaven, I will **exalt my throne** above the stars of God; I will also **sit on the mount** of the congregation on the farthest sides of the north; **I will ascend above the heights of the clouds, I will be like the Most High**.' Yet you shall be brought down to Sheol, To the lowest depths of the Pit. "Those who see you will gaze at you, and consider you, saying: 'Is this the man who made the earth tremble, who shook kingdoms, Who made the world as a wilderness And destroyed its cities, Who did not open the house of his prisoners?' "All the kings of the nations, All of them, sleep in glory, Everyone in his own house; But you are cast out of your grave Like an abominable branch, Like the garment of those who are slain, Thrust through with a sword, Who go down to the stones of the pit, Like a corpse trodden underfoot. You will not be joined with them in burial, because you have destroyed your land and slain your people. The brood of evildoers shall never be named.

The passage commences with the words, "How you have fallen from heaven, O morning star, son of the dawn!" The statement in question pertains to Satan, who previously held the status of an illuminating angel but defied God's divine authority and was subsequently expelled from the heavenly realm. The subsequent text delineates Satan's pride and arrogance, culminating in his rebels against God. Satan aspired to attain divine qualities and dominance over the universe, yet his rebellion proved ineffective.

According to biblical accounts, a significant proportion of heavenly beings, estimated to be one-third, decided to ally themselves with Satan during his rebellion against God, resulting in their expulsion from the heavenly realm alongside him. The repercussions of this cosmic rebellion have had enduring effects on humanity that persist today. According to the Gospel of John, Satan is characterized as the "father of lies" (John 8:44) and the "prince of this world" (John 12:31). His modus operandi involved deceiving and tempting individuals to renounce their faith in God.

The passage of Ezekiel 28:11-19: Moreover the word of the Lord came to me, saying, "Son of man, take up a lamentation for the king of Tyre, and say to him, 'Thus says the Lord God: "You were the seal of perfection, Full of wisdom and perfect in beauty. You were in Eden, the garden of God; Every precious stone was your covering: The sardius, topaz, and diamond, Beryl, onyx, and jasper, Sapphire, turquoise, and emerald with gold. The workmanship of your timbrels and pipes was prepared for you on the day you created. "You were the anointed cherub who covers; I established you; you were on the holy mountain of God; you walked back and forth in the midst of fiery stones. You were perfect in your way from the day you were created until **iniquity** was found in you. "By the abundance of your trading You became filled with **violence** within, and you **sinned**; Therefore, I cast you as a profane thing Out of the mountain of God; And I destroyed you, O covering cherub, From the midst of the fiery stones. "**Your heart was lifted up because of your beauty**; **You corrupted your wisdom for the sake of your splendor**; I cast you to the ground, I laid you before kings, that they might gaze at you. "You defiled your sanctuaries by the multitude of your iniquities, By the iniquity of your trading; Therefore, I brought fire from your midst; It devoured you, And I turned you to ashes upon the earth in the sight of all who saw you. All who knew you among the peoples are astonished at you; You have become a horror, and shall be no more forever."

The biblical account of Ezekiel 28:11-19 pertains to the downfall of the monarch of Tyre. The passage commences with the phrase, "The word of the Lord came to me," followed by a directive to the "Son of man" to express a lamentation regarding the king of Tyre. The Sovereign Lord is quoted as stating that the king of Tyre was an embodiment of perfection and possessed both wisdom and beauty. The scriptural reference in question is Ezekiel 28:11-12. The subsequent section delineates the hubris and conceits of the monarch of Tyre, culminating in his eventual demise.

Nonetheless, numerous academics posit that this excerpt also encompasses a depiction of Satan's descent from the celestial realm. The present interpretation is founded upon the depiction of the monarch of Tyre as being situated "in Eden, the garden of God" (Ezekiel 28:13). As having been "consecrated as a sentinel cherub" (Ezekiel 28:14). The depictions bear a resemblance to the characterizations employed in other biblical passages to portray Satan, as evidenced in Isaiah 14:12-20.

Satan tempts Adam and Eve (Genesis 3): The biblical account of Genesis 3 details Satan's enticement of Adam and Eve within the confines of the Garden of Eden. The text commences with the statement that the serpent possessed greater cunning than any other creature created by the Lord God. The man asked the woman, "Is it true that God has forbidden you from consuming the fruit of any tree in this garden?" (Gen. 3:1). The temptation that Satan presented to Adam and Eve involved the consumption of fruit from the tree of the knowledge of good and evil, an act explicitly prohibited by God. According to the biblical narrative, Satan purportedly enticed the individuals in question with the promise that partaking in the tree's fruit would confer divine qualities and the ability to discern between right and wrong.

Adam and Eve succumbed to the temptation of Satan and consumed the fruit from the Tree of Knowledge, which granted them the ability to discern between good and evil. The act of disobedience committed by the first humans resulted in their expulsion from the Garden of Eden and the subsequent introduction of sin and mortality.

It holds a significant place in Christian theology because of its emphasis on the significance of obedience to God and the perilous nature of temptation. The transgression committed by Adam and Eve resulted in their banishment from the Paradisiacal Garden of Eden, and consequently, the advent of sin and mortality in the world. The act of disobedience can potentially result in downfall.

This is a significant observation as it highlights the necessity for a redeemer. The advent of sin and mortality in the world rendered it unfeasible for humankind to achieve reconciliation with the divine. The process of reconciliation was facilitated by the atoning sacrifice of Jesus Christ on the cross, which effectively overcame the forces of sin and death and enabled us to reconcile with God.

God with Satan over Job: The Book of Job is a biblical narrative that recounts the dialogue between God and Satan concerning the character of Job. In the biblical narrative, Satan challenges God by asserting that Job's devotion to Him is contingent on the blessings of wealth and prosperity that he has received. According to the biblical narrative, Job's faith is tested by Satan with God's permission, resulting in the loss of his wealth, health, and family. Notwithstanding these adversities, Job exhibits unwavering loyalty towards God and refrains from cursing Him.

Spiritual Warfare in the New Testament

Jesus is tempted by Satan: The Bible passage in Luke 4:1-13 recounts the narrative of Jesus undergoing temptation by Satan while in the wilderness. This narrative serves as a potent reminder of the veracity of spiritual conflict and the struggle between righteousness and malevolence. Following his baptism, Jesus was guided by the Holy Spirit to a desert region, where he engaged in a period of fasting for 40 days. During this period, Satan approached Jesus and tempted Him thrice. Initially, the protagonist was enticed to transform stones into bread in order to satiate his hunger. Subsequently, the individual enticed the other with dominion and control over every realm in existence on the condition that he paid homage to Satan. Ultimately, he entices him to verify God's safeguarding by hurling himself off the temple's highest point.

On every occasion, Satan presented temptation to Jesus, the latter of which was countered with scriptural references. The individual cited passages from the book of Deuteronomy, specifically "Man shall not live by bread alone" (Luke 4:4), "You shall worship the Lord your God, and him only shall you serve" (Luke 4:8), and "You shall not put the Lord your God to the test" (Luke 4:12), during their discourse. The narrative of Jesus' temptation by Satan holds great significance for several reasons. Initially, it underscores the reality of spiritual combat and the conflict between good and evil. According to religious beliefs, Satan is considered a tangible adversary whose ultimate goal is to divert individuals from faith in God. Second, this illustrates that Jesus encountered temptation, yet demonstrated unwavering faithfulness to God. This serves as an example for emulation. Third, it serves as a reminder of the significance of comprehending and employing scriptural teaching to combat temptation. Jesus employed the Scriptures as a means of refuting the deceptive statements of Satan.

***Satan prevented Paul from going to Thessalonica*:** The biblical account in Acts 17:1-15 details a missionary expedition to Thessalonica. Nevertheless, prior to his arrival at the intended location, Satan impeded his progress. The following are the essential factors to consider: Paul had just left the Philippines, where he was imprisoned and beaten. Notwithstanding this, he and Silas persisted in disseminating the gospel and preaching to numerous individuals. Subsequently, they journeyed to Thessalonica, a prominent urban center in Macedonia. Upon their arrival in Thessalonica, the individuals proceeded to the synagogue where they commenced preaching to the Jewish community. A portion of the individuals was convinced and aligned with Paul and Silas, whereas others harbored feelings of envy and exhibited opposition towards them. Paul and Silas were accused of instigating turmoil and disrupting the established order. Satan interceded it at this juncture. According to Acts 17:5, the Jews, experiencing feelings of jealousy, assembled a group of wicked individuals from the lower classes of society and incited a disturbance in the city. They proceeded to assault the residence of Jason with the intention of apprehending the targeted individuals and presenting them to an agitated crowd. Paul and Silas were compelled to depart from the urban center and relocate to Berea.

The narrative that Satan impeded Paul's journey to Thessalonica has noteworthy implications for various reasons. Initially, it underscored the veracity of spiritual warfare and the conflict between righteousness and wickedness. An entity known as Satan is a legitimate adversary whose objective is to impede the dissemination of the gospel. Second, even individuals deeply committed to serving God may encounter resistance and hindrances. Despite engaging in God's work, Paul and Silas encountered persecution and were compelled to escape for safety. Third, it serves as a reminder of the significance of persistence and faith in divine plans. Notwithstanding this resistance, Paul and Silas persisted in disseminating the gospel and affecting numerous conversions.

Conclusion

Even now, the cosmic wars that began in heaven between Christ and Satan continue. The conflict is not just between Christ and the devil; the adversary has gone farther in his wicked conspiracy to destroy God's most valuable possession, His Creation—Humans (Deut 26:18; James 1:18). Satan is determined to go to any extreme to destroy humankind who was made in "God's image" (Gen 1:27). Therefore, Lord established a boundary between good and evil, helping to ensure that his creations would be secure. However, the reverse is true. The devil deceitfully swindles Adam and Eve, our first parents to eat from the forbidden tree and humiliate God by showing how His creation decided to reject God and appear as if they were partners with Satan's legion. For this reason, God in His infinite wisdom declared, "And I will put enmity between you and the woman, and between your seed and her seed; he shall bruise your head, and you shall bruise his heel" (Gen 3:15).

People are prone to blaming the devil to absolve their guilt, rationalize their actions, and avoid the consequences of their own sins. Although the originator of sin may be the devil, we no longer blame the devil for our sins. The notion that "the devil made me do it," is nothing but ignorance of God's words.

When confronted with her transgression in the garden of Eden, Eve responds in a similar manner by blaming the serpent. Adam, too, pretended as victim and blamed Eve and even the Lord, claiming that "the woman made me do it, the one you gave me" (Gen 3:12). Certainly, Satan encouraged the temptation as the deceiver and liar, but Eve replied with unbelief and disobedience, and Adam failed to fulfil his responsibilities as the head of his household. So, what can be done?

In the following chapters, a gradual exploration of the devil will be undertaken, focusing on discerning his identity and modus operandi. The extensive discourse presented in the subsequent chapters will provide us with the necessary knowledge and motivation to equip ourselves for spiritual warfare against the adversary from a divine perspective.

Chapter 2

Know Your Enemy

> *"You are of God, little children, and have overcome them, because He who is in you is greater than he who is in the world."*
> ***I John 4:4***

The previous section examined the cosmic struggle that profoundly affected the correlation between humanity and divinity. Moreover, because of this phenomenon, humanity is currently engaged in spiritual warfare, which has significant implications. This conflict possesses the capacity to eradicate human existence and impede one's ability to experience divine intervention and the corresponding redemptive plans that God has in store for them. Owing to the accomplishments of Jesus, we can confront this conflict with a sense of victory. Nonetheless, it is imperative that we exercise prudence in addressing the matter of our adversary, namely, the devil, and acquire a comprehensive understanding of his nature, lest we succumb to disorder.

In Colossians 2:15, Paul asserts that, through crucifixion, Jesus effectively disarmed principalities and powers, publicly exhibiting His triumph over them. The powers alluded to by Paul in Ephesians 6:12 are likely spiritual authorities. Paul's intention is not related to disregard for secular leaders and authorities. Instead, he refers to Jesus' authority over the powers of spiritual darkness (Rendell, 2010).

The scope of spiritual warfare extends beyond the realms of demonization or the deliverance ministry, as noted by Kraft (2016) and Coleman (2015).

The prevalence of spiritual warfare exceeds our initial assumptions, and instances of demonic oppression are frequently attributed to peculiar life occurrences. Spiritual warfare is a continuing phenomenon that occurs in daily life, as noted by Wood (2018). This chapter seeks to clarify the identity of the enemy referred to in the Bible, which includes designations such as "false slanderer," "accuser," "liar," and "murderer." What is the origin of this evil entity? What is his underlying purpose or objective? What was the basis of his function? Who is part of the devil's army? Who is commonly referred to as our demon?

Who are Demons?

Learning about the devil was intentional in this book. However, studying demonology[1] does not divert the central theme of this book, that is, glorifying God in the battle of spiritual warfare. Demonology holds immense significance, whether it is examined as a branch of revealed theology within the biblical context or as a phase of the broader study of religion outside it. The ramifications of this phenomenon are significant and extend far beyond the confines of biblical texts (Unger 1994). Even though biblical demonology is vital in the field of Christian theology as well as in the field of comparative religion, the problem and perplexities that surround it are unquestionably significant and stimulate careful research and investigation to find a solution (Unger, 1994).

Demons are real, and their existence is real. Different cultures and religions have their own interpretations and definitions of demon. N. N. Bhattacharyya, in his work "*Indian Demonology: The Inverted Pantheon*," discusses demonology as it appears in Indian Vedic, Buddhist, Jain, epic, and Puranic literature. The book delves deeply into folklore and stories surrounding a wide variety of demonic beings that can exist in the cosmos,

1 The field of study that pertains to the examination of demons as they are portrayed in religious belief and myth is known as demonology. The term can encompass various fields, such as theology, religious doctrine, or occultism, contingent upon the context. The examination of a hierarchical structure of malevolent supernatural beings is a subject of interest in numerous religious traditions.

sky, and land. According to the author, one of the reasons why Indian demonology is so expansive is that India is home to over 300 distinct tribes, each of which has a mythology that includes gods, demons, and spirits (Bhattacharyya, 2000).

The subject of demonology in Hinduism is both intricate and diverse. The perception of demons in Hinduism is not homogeneous; however, they are commonly regarded as potent supernatural entities capable of inflicting harm on human beings. In Hindu mythology, supernatural entities known as demons are commonly identified as *assuras*, *rakshasas*, or *daityas*. They are portrayed as possessing a diverse array of powers and capabilities.

An image of Asura

Certain demons possess malevolent and wicked traits, whereas others exhibit a degree of ambiguity and may evoke sympathy. Within certain Hindu traditions, demons are perceived as symbolic representations of the more negative facets of human behavior, including but not limited to greed, jealousy, and anger. The concept of demonic possession holds significant importance in Hinduism as it is attributed to the influence of evil spirits or entities. The concept of possession can be interpreted in several ways. It may be perceived as a punishment for past transgressions or as a trial of one's religious conviction and mechanism for personal spiritual advancement.

In Islamic religion, demons are potent forces that reflect the battle between the eternal principles of good and evil. Demons are supernatural creatures that are often referred to as Jinns, Ghuls, and other similar beings (Basharin, 2009). Within Islamic faith, demons are regarded as dark entities that symbolize the ongoing struggle between the two eternal principles of good and evil. These paranormal entities are frequently denoted as *Jinns*, *Ghuls*, or similar entities.

Ravana is depicted as a Rakshasa (Demon)

The Quran is the primary source of depictions of the indigenous supernatural beings of central Arabia, both prior to and following the emergence of Islam. The belief in spirits remains ingrained in the minds of Sunda Muslims in Indonesia, stemming from their adherence to traditional customs and teachings of Islam. The notion of the existence of spirits is widely acknowledged as a factual phenomenon, specifically referring to the *lelembut*, which are supernatural entities that predate human beings, encompassing deities, malevolent entities, and supernatural beings known as *dedemit* (Kasmana et. al. 2018, 11). The portrayal of the devil in Ottoman miniature art involves the depiction of various entities, such as fire-breathing dragons, scorpions, snakes, Malik, and *zebani* (demons) of hell, which are consistent with Islamic faith and literature (Harman 2016, 1065).

Ten types of *Jinn* in Islamic beliefs

According to Buddhism, demons are dwellers of hell who intend to torment, tempt, and thwart people's efforts to achieve enlightenment (Strickmann 2002). Buddhism presents a distinctive viewpoint on demonology, akin to several other religious traditions. According to Buddhism's tenets, demons are hell inhabitants who seek to inflict suffering, entice, and obstruct individuals in their pursuit of enlightenment. In Buddhist art and literature, demons are frequently portrayed as formidable and repulsive beings with numerous heads, arms, and legs. Certain negative emotions or mental states such as anger, jealousy, or desire are occasionally linked to them.

According to Buddhist cosmology, there are six distinct realms of existence, one of which is the realm inhabited by hell beings or demons. According to this belief, these entities were purported to undergo profound anguish because of their unfavorable karma and conduct in previous incarnations. According to popular beliefs, demons are perceived as extrinsic entities capable of exerting an impact on human conduct, ultimately causing individuals to deviate from the righteous path. By contrast, certain belief systems emphasize that demons are representations of the psyche and surmounting them necessitates internal metamorphosis and spiritual discipline.

Buddhist tradition encompasses the notion of Mara within its demonology, which is believed to have tempted the Buddha through the manifestation of pleasure-seeking delights and material achievements. Mara is commonly regarded as a representation of the hindrances that impede individuals from attaining enlightenment. Apart from demons, Buddhism acknowledges other paranormal entities including deities, specters, and famous spirits. It is widely postulated that these entities occupy diverse planes of being and possess varying levels of potency and sway over the human matter.

Demon King *Mara* of the Sixth Realm in Buddhism

It is noteworthy that perceptions of demons in the western community are very different from those in the east. Marko Kolic, in his article, reports that 57 percent of people in the United States believe that Satan is not real but a symbol of evil. He further mentions, "Even more alarming, 46 percent of Evangelicals and 65 percent of Catholics in America believe that Satan is either not real or simply a symbol (Barna)" (Kolic, 2009).

Although the definitions of demons, evils, and related notions vary depending on the context, we must accept that they exist and that their desire to separate us from God's providence is real. Furthermore, a devil's attempt to pull us away from God has many effects on humans. As a result, it is imperative that we recognize the demons around us. These demons do not always take physical form, but they can still impact us, even when we are unaware of it—both inside and outside.

Demons in the Bible

When it comes to Demons in the Bible, they are often mentioned. There are several references to demons in the Bible. Therefore, who are these demons and what do they do?

The word "demon" is derived from the Greek word daimon, which means "spirit" or "ghost." In the Bible, demons are fallen angels cast out of heaven because of their rebellion against God, and they are evil spirits who roam the earth looking for people to possess and control (Theology Today, 2019). The idea that demons can enter a person's body through things such as open wounds or living in their house is not meant to be taken literally. It is more like saying that when people are sick or their homes lack faith, they might be opening the door to negative influences. Once inside a person's mind, they can cause problems, such as physical illnesses, mental disorders, and demonic possession.

In the previous chapter, it was stated that evil forces brought about cosmic conflict and disrupted the divine communion with the Almighty. Given our prior discussion of the existence of demons in different world religions, it would be reasonable to delve into the biblical perspective of this subject matter. In the following discussion, we will review biblical passages that expound on demons to varying degrees.

Old Testament

In the Old Testament, the way demons are described shows the importance of understanding what people believe about them. Knowing these beliefs helps us identify symbolic ideas that impact our lives. Recognizing evil forces in our midst can prompt us to take measures to overcome them through individual transformation and spiritual practice, a principle that is essential in Christian faith. In Christianity, the fundamental idea involves accepting Jesus, repenting, and leading a godly life to undergo a transformative experience. Therefore, studying demonology provides important insights into how humans face encounters with evil forces and the strategies they should embrace to comprehend and confront these phenomena over time, guided by God.

In Hebrew, there does not exist a lexical equivalent to the English term "demon," nor does any term convey the identical connotation of an evil entity operating under Satan to annihilate humanity. The New Testament refers to demons as spiritual entities that are hostile toward God and possess the ability to afflict humans. The demons are described as causing physical ailments and spiritual impurity, as indicated by the recurring label "unclean." Pertejo and López (2022) explored the instances of demonic possessions involving Judas and Mary Magdalene, significant characters in the New Testament. Both experienced demonic possessions, with Jesus conducting exorcism to alleviate their conditions (1).

The Old Testament encompasses the concept of demonology, which reflects its multifaceted and varied nature in diverse cultural and historical settings. They are portrayed as luring individuals into transgressions and diverting them from a moral uprightness. The term utilized in the Old Testament to refer to demons or devil as שֵׁד (shêd) or *shade*, originating from the Hebrew language. The Old Testament mentions the devil, a distinct entity in Christian theology that refers to Satan and Lucifer. The devil is commonly perceived as the personification of evil and frequently portrayed as enticing individuals to engage in sinful behavior, thereby diverting them from a virtuous course.

The passage in Deuteronomy 32:16-17 shows Israelites engaging in worshiping demonic entities. This account is situated in the Old Testament. The passage reads (emphasis added), "They provoked Him [God] to jealousy with foreign gods with abominations they provoked Him [God] to anger. They sacrificed to demons, not to God, to gods they did not know, to new gods, new arrivals that your fathers did not fear" (Deut 32:16-17). This passage reflects the significance of appropriate worship and the potential risks associated with participating in spiritual rituals that deviate from the divine plan. The significance of acknowledging the symbolic importance of demons and their associated beliefs is highlighted as a crucial aspect of spiritually enriching life in loyalty to God.

2 Chronicles 11:15 defines the process of appointing priests and Levites for the purpose of rendering service in the temple, as documented in the Old Testament. The passage highlights the significance of appropriate worship and the potential hazards of participating in spiritual rituals that deviate from God's will. It highlights the relevance of understanding the symbolism of demons and the associated beliefs to live a spiritually satisfying existence.

Leviticus 17:7 (NIV) "They must no longer offer sacrifices to the goat idols to whom they prostitute themselves. This is to be a lasting ordinance for them and for the generations to come." This passage warns against offering sacrifices to false gods, hinting at the spiritual dangers associated with idolatry.

Psalm 106:35-37 (NIV), "but they mingled with the nations and adopted their customs. They worshiped their idols, which became snares to them. They sacrificed their sons and their daughters to false gods." This passage reflects on Israelites adopting the customs of other nations, including idol worship, which is portrayed as spiritually harmful.

In Isaiah 8:19-20, "When someone tells you to consult mediums and spiritists, who whisper and mutter, should not a people inquire of their God? Why consult the dead on behalf of the living? Consult God's instruction and the testimony of warning. If anyone does not speak according to this word, they have no light of dawn." Isaiah discourages seeking guidance from mediums and spiritists, emphasizing the importance of seeking guidance from God's instructions.

Samuel 16:14-16 (NIV), "Now the Spirit of the Lord had departed from Saul, and an evil spirit from the Lord tormented him. Saul's attendants said to him, 'See, an evil spirit from God is tormenting you. Let our lord command his servants to search for someone who can play a lyre. He will play when the evil spirit from God comes on you, and you will feel better.'" In this passage, an evil spirit is troubling King Saul, and music is suggested as a remedy for soothing him. This may indicate a connection between disobedience and the presence of a malevolent spirit.

Deuteronomy 18:9-12 (NIV), "When you enter the land the Lord your God is giving you, do not learn to imitate the detestable ways of the nations there. Let no one be found among you who sacrifices their son or daughter in the fire, who practices divination or sorcery, interprets omens, engages in witchcraft, or casts spells, or who is a medium or spiritist or who consults the dead." This passage warns against various practices, including divination and sorcery, and suggests the recognition of spiritual dangers associated with certain activities.

While these passages may not explicitly mention demons, they contribute to the Old Testament's broader narrative of the dangers of straying from God's commandments and engaging in practices associated with false gods or demons.

New Testament

In the New Testament, the concept of demons is developed more explicitly, and there are numerous references to demonic possession, exorcism, and the activities of evil spirits. The New Testament includes references to demons, which are considered threatening supernatural beings capable of inflicting harm on human beings. In the New Testament, διάβολος *diabolos* is the term for demon or devil, frequently used synonymously with "unclean spirit," indicating the conviction that demons were linked with impurity and transgression. In various accounts, Jesus is portrayed as performing exorcism and underscoring his authority over evil entities.

The New Testament mentions Satan, regarded as the embodiment of evil, and is frequently portrayed as drawing individuals towards sin and diverting them from the course of moral uprightness. The study of demons in the New Testament shows the necessity of correct worship and perils of engaging in spiritual practices that are contrary to God's purpose. This underscores the significance of acknowledging the symbolic connotations of demons and related convictions in attaining spiritual contentment. The depictions of demons in the New Testament emphasize the significance of acknowledging the destructiveness of evil entities and the imperative of relying on divine power to overcome them.

The biblical account in Luke 8:2 pertains to the exorcism of demons by Jesus Christ by a woman identified as Mary Magdalene. The passage states that a group of women who had previously been afflicted with evil spirits and physical ailments, including a woman named Mary Magdalene, who had seven demons, healed. This passage highlights the relevance of recognizing the destructive nature of evil powers and the necessity of depending on divine power to overcome them. The text underscores the significance of true worship and the risks associated with indulging in beliefs that deviate from the divine purposes.

1 Corinthians 10:20 elucidates the hazardous consequences of engaging in idol worship. The excerpt asserts that the offerings made by the gentiles are directed towards malevolent entities rather than benevolent ones. Thus, engaging in any form of association with such entities is unadvisable. This passage highlights the significance of appropriate worship and the perils associated with participating in spiritual rituals that deviate from the divine plan. The significance of acknowledging the symbolic importance of demons and related beliefs is underscored as a means of achieving spiritual fulfillment.

Matthew 4:24 (NIV), "News about him spread all over Syria, and people brought to him all who were ill with various diseases, those suffering severe pain, the demon-possessed, those having seizures, and the paralyzed; and he healed them." This verse is just one example of many in the Gospels where Jesus is portrayed as healing the demon-possessed, indicating a belief in the presence of evil spirits that cause afflictions.

Mark 5:1-20 tells the story of the demon-possessed man in the region of the Gerasenes, where Jesus performs an exorcism, casting the demons into a herd of pigs. Luke 10:17-20 (NIV), "The seventy-two returned with joy and said, 'Lord, even the demons submit to us in your name.'" This passage reflects the authority given by Jesus to his disciples over demons in his name.

Acts 16:16-18 (NIV), "Once when we were going to the place of prayer, we were met by a female slave who had a spirit by which she predicted the future. She earned a great deal of money to her owners through fortune-telling. She followed Paul and the rest of us, shouting, 'These men are servants of the Most High God, who are telling you the way to be saved.'" This account highlights encounters with individuals possessed by spirits and the distinction between the spirits within them and the message proclaimed by Paul.

Ephesians 6:12 (NIV), "For our struggle is not against flesh and blood, but against the rulers, against the authorities, against the powers of this dark world and against the spiritual forces of evil in the heavenly realms." This verse from the Ephesians speaks to spiritual warfare against evil forces, acknowledging a hierarchy of spiritual entities.

In the New Testament, the understanding of demons as malevolent spiritual beings that influence and possess individuals becomes more explicit. The Gospels showcase Jesus' authority over demons through his teachings and exorcism. Later, New Testament writings, such as the epistles, also acknowledge the existence of spiritual forces and the need for believers to be vigilant in their faith.

After briefly exploring the concept of demons, the subsequent focus shifts to recognizing demons that exert both direct and indirect influences on us. At this point, acknowledging that we exist within a cosmic battle and having aligned ourselves with God, it becomes imperative to identify "who is my demon?" It is crucial to clarify that stating this does not imply active possession by demons but rather acknowledges their influences that directly or indirectly impact us. Understanding our demon(s)—acknowledging that there may be more than one—positions us in confronting and engaging in spiritual warfare against these influences. Numerous scholarly works have extensively explored, analyzed, and provided guidance on participation in both the visible and invisible aspects of spiritual warfare. The primary goal of this book is to acknowledge the presence of demons. While this idea may be uncomfortable to some, it is an undeniable reality that every individual grapples with inner demons. The concept of inner demons does not necessarily involve active spirit possession or demonization; rather, it can be described as a form of passive demonic influence that affects our thoughts and behaviors. As we delve into the enigmatic and often-overlooked realm of the devil, our aim is to achieve a profound comprehension of these demons.

Who is my Demon?

Christianity acknowledges the presence of demons, signifying a belief in an evil spirit. However, there is not much detailed explanation suggesting that each person has a particular demon or set of demons that exclusively influences and dominates them. Instead, the emphasis is on the broader recognition of the existence of evil forces, with the understanding that individuals may encounter and contend with these evil powers. Unfortunately, many Christians tend to view the struggle against such forces as a collective and universal endeavor rather than personalized domination by specific demons. However, many Christians also emphasize the repercussions of the power wielded by evil forces, underscoring the importance of seeking divine strength to overcome these influences in their personal lives.

Inner demons are negative thoughts and messages that do not seem to shake off. They often repeat in our minds, creating a not-so-happy dialogue. These thoughts may say things like, "You are not good enough" or "You cannot do this." They are little voices that affect how we feel about ourselves and the world around us. These voices create delusions to put fear, anxiety, jealousy, etc. in our minds that ultimately drive us away from God.

Recognizing these inner demons is therefore important. Once we are aware of them, we can work on changing the negative dialogue. It is like taking control and telling those thoughts, “I am good enough” or “I can do this.” Seeking support from friends, family, church, and spiritual disciplines, such as fasting and praying, can help overcome these inner struggles. The journey is about understanding, confronting, and ultimately finding a more positive and uplifting way to train ourselves to resist demonic power.

Before identifying the inner demons that we may be intentionally or unintentionally struggling with, it is imperative to develop a comprehensive understanding of the diverse forms of evil spirit that coexist within our surroundings. Despite their widespread presence, we often dismiss them as mere reflections of an individual’s disposition or responses to a given circumstance. There are several concepts to consider when it comes to understanding individuals who deal with health challenges, personal hardships, social dynamics, religious affiliations, and other related issues.

According to scientific research, nightmares are inherently distressing and can impede their ability to achieve restorative sleep. Moreover, they have been found to exhibit an associated with various psychiatric issues. The occurrence of nightmares is often linked to negative emotions that arise from stressful events. Consequently, nightmares have been studied primarily in the context of post-traumatic stress disorder (PTSD) (Rek et al. 2017, 1123).

Secular cultures provide a range of viewpoints on inner demons, but the Bible and the book’s discussion of cosmic conflict propose that every person is involved in an inner struggle with demonic forces. Recognizing the nature of the enemy of God is crucial to waging a war against it. Satan is commonly regarded as the adversary of God, whose primary objective is to tempt individuals to deviate from their spiritual connections with the divine. He achieves this by presenting the allure of desirable worldly things such as wealth, power, and prestige. Moreover, he strives to convince them that they fail to uphold divine standards of acceptance. God expects people to accept Jesus as their personal savior, and this is referred to as the divine standard. The devil's plan is not to confront God directly but rather to undermine his creation by attacking their character and insulting them. This is an attempt to prove that God has made a mistake by creating humans. Satan, infamous for his duplicitous nature and penchant for falsehoods, employs numerous strategies to deter individuals from acknowledging and adhering to God's teachings (Piper 2016).

Whoever stands in opposition to God, and His will for our lives can be considered an enemy of God. This includes Satan and his demons, but also includes anyone who tempts us to wander from the path God has laid for us. Every one of us struggles with our demon(s), which works against us to prevent us from doing what God considers right and good. To triumph over this foe, we must recognize Satan as our adversary and engage in combat against him with God's power.

We all have our demons. The voices in our heads constantly tell us that we are not good enough and will never amount to anything significant in the world. The uncertainties and worries that we have to prohibit us from taking chances and going towards our goals. These inner demons are our deadliest foes and prevent us from living the life we were meant to live the fullest. Nevertheless, we have the opportunity to secure dominance over them, put an end to their voices, triumph over our phobias and vanquish our demons. We have the ability to control our destiny; if you want to find out who your demon is, ask yourself this question:

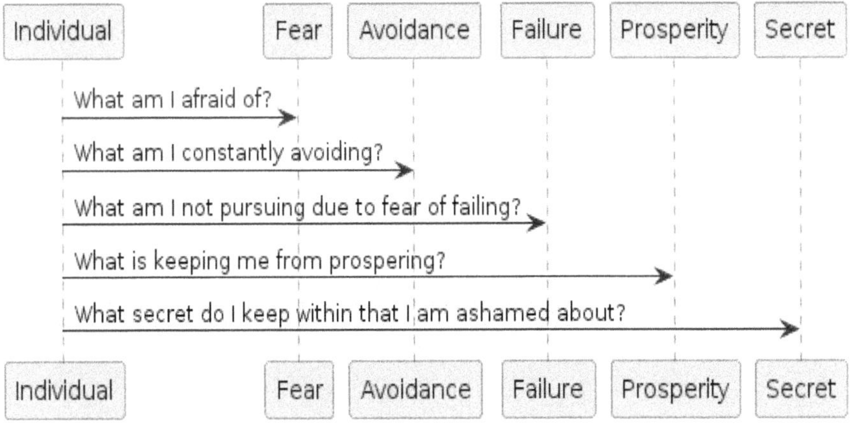

Your answers have shed light on your inner demon. Once you have identified your adversary, you can begin working on a plan to overpower it. Nevertheless, what if we can recognize these evil forces and determine how to subdue them? In the following section, we investigate the concept of the "inner devil" and discuss strategies for overcoming it.

What is an inner demon?

In addition to the complete takeover by demons, which is referred to as demonization, several other forms of demonic activity are not always apparent. These activities can take many shapes and forms, and negative thoughts or beliefs about oneself can be considered inner demons.

An internal adversary impedes its ability to reach its full potential and achieve its objectives. Inner demons can have many different forms. Sometimes, the battles you fight within your own thoughts can be referred to as an "inner demon." This may have been triggered by experiences that instilled a limiting belief in you, causing you to conceal a part of yourself to appear normal. Alternatively, it may have arisen from circumstances that led you to believe that you needed to conceal a part of yourself, causing you to behave differently and appear normal.

It is an inner concept, set of thoughts, or understanding about life that, when spoken, appears simple for others to deal with, but when you try to work around it, manifest past it, or simply be alone with it, you feel in conflict with your mind.

For example, you may have a demon telling you that you are not good enough or will never amount to anything, and this demon may prevent you from taking risks, pursuing your dreams, or overcoming life challenges or addictions. Another example of an inner demon is when fear is both an emotion and a cognition that people instinctively experience when perceiving a threat to their well-being. Fearful thoughts and feelings develop whenever we believe that something will damage or threaten our happiness or security. These thoughts and sentiments, influenced by inner demons, paralyze our capacity to act authoritatively. The following diagram is another example of an inner demon that includes perfectionism and procrastination:

Perfectionism is at the heart of the diagram and can lead to self-doubt, fear of failure, fear of achievement, and fear of change. These anxieties can then lead to procrastination, which can feed on perfectionism and the self-doubt cycle.

Examples of inner demons include the following.

These negative beliefs can become so ingrained in our thinking that they influence how we view the world around us and ourselves. They make us feel confined, helpless, and isolated. However, it is imperative to remember that these are merely thoughts and do not represent reality in any way. In addition, we have the potential to bring about the necessary changes to the inner demons.

We cannot ignore that there are demonic beings in the world. In Bradfield (2012), C.S. Lewis rightly said, "Humanity falls into two equal and opposite errors concerning the Devil. Either they take him altogether too seriously, or they do not take him seriously enough" (71). The first thing you need to do to conquer your inner demon is to recognize that you have one. To get started, set aside some time to think about the negative thoughts and beliefs that you have about yourself and give them some thoughts. If writing things down helps, do that. Once you have recognized your inner demon, you may proceed to the next step.

Ask yourself: Is this really true? Do I have evidence to support this belief? Is there another way to examine this?

Biblical Demons

One of the most common questions people ask about demons is, "Who is my demon?" The short answer is that we do not know it. The Bible does not provide a list of demons linked to specific people. There are, however, a few verses that offer insights into the possible ways in which devils carry out their activities. Jesus explains in Luke 11:24-26 that when an evil spirit is cast out of a person, the spirit will roam through dry lands looking for a place to rest. According to this, demons do not appear to have a specific prey in mind; instead, they wander aimlessly until they discover someone prone to possession or weakness.

Another text can be gleaned from the passage in Matthew 12:43–45, in which Jesus explains that a demon exorcised from a person will attempt to return with seven other demons that are even more evil and take control of that person immediately. This indicates that demons feel more secure when they possess large groups of humans; thus, it is likely that they will work together to take over as many people as possible.

Mark 5:9 recounts the account of a man possessed by a legion of demons. One individual can be possessed by various demons simultaneously, much like a legion, a Roman military formation consisting of approximately 6,000 troops.

According to Mark 5:1–20, evil spirits shudder in the thought of Jesus. This is because Jesus possesses the authority to expel and condemn them to an eternity of torment (Matthew 25:41). Demons are aware that they will meet their end if Jesus captures them. Consequently, they will do whatever they can evade Him.

Additionally, sickness and disease are frequently associated with demons. Jesus cures a man in Matthew 12:22 who had been afflicted by a demon, which had caused him to be blind and mute. Jesus casts out a spirit that had been tormenting a woman for eighteen years, restoring her full mobility (Luke 13:11-13). Furthermore, the passage in Acts 16:16-18 describes how Paul exorcises a demon from a slave girl who had been giving her master false prophesies so that he could gain money off of them.

We can see that our demons are fallen angels wishing to do us harm, and will take advantage of whatever opportunity they can find. However, we do not know the specific identities of demons. We also see that Jesus possesses the authority to guard us against them and expel them from us if they successfully take possession of us (Texada, 2012; Ingram, 2015). In Christianity, devils and demons are closely associated with sins through various mechanisms. The devil is often portrayed as a tempter, luring individuals towards sinful acts, as seen in biblical accounts of temptation. Additionally, these evil entities are considered active participants in spiritual warfare, working to lead people away from righteousness and towards sinful behavior. Their influence is depicted as deceptive, distorting moral values, and encouraging disobedience. In some cases, demons are thought to possess individuals, compelling them to commit sinful acts. The devil's rebellion against God, often rooted in pride, is a symbolic representation of the epitome of sin. Overall, the association between devil, demons, and sins underscores the moral and ethical dimensions inherent in the struggle between good and evil within religious frameworks.

Now that we have acknowledged that the devil is believed to prompt humans to sin, with the ultimate goal of separating us from God, let us delve into the concept of sins, as presented in the Bible. While the Bible addresses sin in various passages, let us specifically explore the seven deadly sins highlighted in its teachings.

The Seven Deadly Sins

While the Bible itself does not explicitly list the seven deadly sins as a collective concept, these sins, popularized by Pope Gregory I in 600 A.D. within Roman Catholic theology, align closely with the notions of the Devil and his schemes against humanity. There are seven deadly sins: Pride, Greed, Lust, Envy, Gluttony, Wrath, and Sloth. Each of these factors can lead to a spiritual death. These sins are often called capital vices or cardinal sins because they are the roots of all other vices.

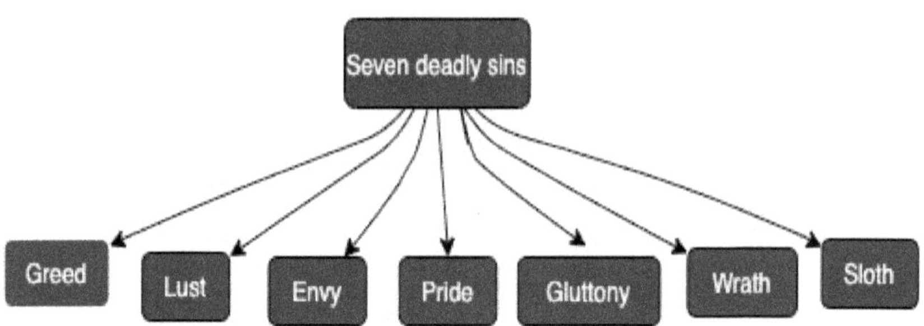

First, Pride is a deadly sin of thinking too highly about oneself. This is often called the sin of arrogance or conceits. This leads to a lack of humility and inflated sense of self-importance. Pride is the root of all other evils, because it leads us to believe that we are better than others and do not need or acknowledge God. Pride is excessive love for the self. It is thought that you are better than others and deserve more than them. Pride leads to self-righteousness and judgmental attitudes. The sin led to Satan's fall from heaven (Isaiah 14:12-15).

Second, the Greed is the deadly sin of wanting. This is also known as avarice or covetousness. Greed leads to a never-ending cycle of desire and dissatisfaction. Greed leads to theft, fraud, and materialism. The sin led to Judas's betrayal of Jesus (Matthew 26:14-16). It can also lead to hoarding and lack of generosity. Greed is an insatiable desire for more and never being content with what one has. It leads to theft, fraud, and other crimes and is the root of all materialism. "For the love of money is a root of all kinds of evil, for which some have strayed from the faith in their greediness, and pierced themselves through with many sorrows" (1 Timothy 6:10).

Third, Lust is the deadly sin of uncontrolled sexual desire. This is often called lechery or sensuality. Lust leads to a preoccupation with sex and obsession with physical pleasure. This can also lead to promiscuity, adultery, and other sexual sins. Lust is the excessive love of pleasure, an uncontrolled desire for things that are not rightful. Lust leads to adultery, pornography, and other obscenic sexual acts. It can lead to adultery, pornography, masturbation, and other sexual behaviors. Lust can also cause people to objectify others and see them as nothing more than sexual objects. This is the same sin that culminates in David's extramarital relationship with Bathsheba. (2 Samuel 11:2-5).

Fourth, Envy is the deadly sin of wanting what others have. It is also known as jealousy or covetousness. *Envy* can be defined as an excessive love for one's own or another's possession. It is an unhealthy desire for other people's possessions and the root cause of backbiting, slander, and caustic behavior. This sin led to Cain's murder of Abel (Genesis 4:3-8). Envy wants what someone else has, leading to jealousy, resentment, and sometimes violence. Envy is often mistaken for admiration, but there are two different things. Admiring someone motivates you to be like them, and envy motivates you to tear them down.

Fifth, Gluttony is the deadly sin of overindulgence. Excessive love for food and drink, dissipation, and waste of resources lead to obesity, alcoholism, and drug addiction. This transgression resulted in Lot's wife becoming a pillar of salt (Genesis 19:26). The earliest apparent case of gluttony in the

Bible occurs in the life of that 'profane' person, "Esau, who for one morsel of meat sold his birthright" (Heb 12:16). Esau's reaction demonstrates why Jacob was legitimate heir. To begin, he was overdramatic when he said he was going to die. He was not going to starve because he could not eat his lentil soup (Butkiewicz 2020). This was just an act of gluttony.

Sixth, Wrath is the excessive desire for revenge. The deadly sin of wrath is extreme love for revenge. This can lead to anger, hatred, or violence. One of the seven deadly sins is rage, which is sometimes an overwhelming desire for vengeance. "You shall not take vengeance, nor bear any grudge against the children of your people, but you shall love your neighbor as yourself: I am the LORD" (Leviticus 19:18). God says, "Beloved, do not avenge yourselves, but rather give place to wrath; for it is written, "Vengeance is Mine, I will repay," says the Lord" (Romans 12:19). There is a risk that this will spark hostility and, perhaps, victimization. The term "wrath" in the Bible can have different meanings depending on the context. When referring to human wrath, the Bible often portrays it as a negative and potentially destructive emotion, cautioning against harmful consequences. For instance, verses such as Proverbs 15:1 highlight the importance of managing and avoiding human wraths. However, when the term is associated with God, it signifies His righteous anger in response to sin and disobedience. In this context, God's wrath is considered just and necessary, reflecting God's divine nature. An example is found in Romans 1:18, which states that the wrath of God is revealed against godlessness and wickedness. Therefore, while the Bible discourages human wrath because of its potential for harm, God's wrath is portrayed as a justified response to human wrongdoing, illustrating His commitment to justice and holiness.

Seventh, the sloth is a sin that is often associated with laziness. However, the definition of sloth goes beyond being lazy. Sloth is also characterized by apathy and a lack of motivation. It can be challenging to overcome sloths because it is easy to become content while doing nothing. The Bible has much to say about sloth and its detrimental effect on our relationship with God. For example, Proverbs 6:6-8 says, "Go to the ant, you sluggard; consider its ways and be wise! It has no commander, overseer, or ruler yet stores its provisions in summer and gathers its food at harvest." In other words, even simple creatures can work hard and be productive. We should consider this as a reminder that we must do the same.

While Demons are certainly powerful beings, we see throughout the Bible that Jesus was even more powerful. He had complete authority over them and could cast them out with a simple command. So, if you are ever faced with a demon, remember that you have nothing to fear. Just can set you free. This approach is effective when we carefully acknowledge our shortcomings and surrender our supplication to God's throne of grace for mercy, seeking divine benevolence through repentance. Therefore, we can effectively recognize and confront our inner demons by acknowledging their limitations, difficulties, hardships, and transgressions.

Identifying my Sin, Identifying my Demons

Let us establish that we all have demons that we battle daily. Whether procrastination, fear, or insecurity, we all have something that holds us back from being our best selves. How do you identify your demons? Moreover, once you have identified them, how do you battle them? First, it is essential to understand that everyone has a different demon. What might be a demon for one person may not be a demon for another person. Our demons were based on individual experiences, values, and beliefs. Therefore, the first step in identifying your demons is to take some time to reflect on your life and what has led you to where you are today. What things have held you back in the past? What are the factors that make you feel anxious or insecure? Once you understand your personal history, you will be in a better position to identify your demons.

Once you have identified your demons, the next step is to deal with them. This requires some introspection and honest self-reflection. What are the factors that trigger your demons? What are the factors that make them feel more powerful? Once you have a good understanding of your triggers, you can begin to work on developing coping mechanisms. This might involve seeking help, developing positive self-talk, or finding healthy outlets for emotions. A church group, pastor, friends, or family is ideal to seek support. The most important thing is to find what works for you and to be patients with yourself. Dealing with demons is not an overnight process; however, various strategies and practices can assist individuals in effectively managing their challenges and fostering their overall well-being.

First, take some time to think about things that prevent you from achieving your goals or living a happy life. What are the things that hold you back? Make a list of these things and then ask yourself why they hold such power over you. Is this because you are afraid of failing? Or is it because you are not confident in your ability to succeed? Once you have identified your demons, it is time to start fighting them. The best way to do this is to face your fear of the head-on. If you are afraid of failing, start taking risks and putting oneself in situations where failure is possible. If you are not confident in your ability to succeed, start taking steps to improve your skills and knowledge. The more demons you face, the weaker they will become. The more you face your demons, the weaker their hold over you will become.

For example, procrastination is one of the most common demon possessions. "I will read the Bible tomorrow," "I will pray later," I will go to church next time" are some common Christian procrastinations. People often find themselves putting off tasks they do not really want to do, even though they know they need them. To deal with this, one method is that we can start using a technique called "time blocking." This involves setting aside specific blocks of time to work on certain tasks. Individuals can effectively manage their time and maintain focus by allocating dedicated time slots to different tasks, thereby minimizing potential distractions. To address procrastination, it is imperative to establish a comprehensive plan.

Effective strategies for overcoming procrastination include identifying peak productivity periods, grouping similar tasks together, breaking tasks into shorter intervals, using a calendar or planner for Bible reading, avoiding multitasking, and taking regular breaks. In addition to time blocking, individuals can employ additional techniques such as enhancing self-awareness, setting clear and specific goals, implementing effective time management, maintaining motivation, and using positive self-talk to reward themselves for accomplishments.

The Devil's Plot Against Us

Sin is a scheme devised by Satan with the intention of causing our downfall and leading us away from God, resulting in subsequent despair. Sin is something that lurks on every one of us, and it is up to each of us to find a way to triumph over it. To achieve this, we can acknowledge our wrongdoings, change our sinful behavior, and seek forgiveness for our past mistakes.

Satan employs the sense to which we are most attentive, whether it be sight, sound, touch, smell, or taste, to lure us into temptation. According to God, our senses are excellent (Ps 115:3-8; Prov 20:12; Matt 13:16). He gave them to us so we could enjoy them within his set limits. However, if we deviate from the purpose God has for us, they become an attempt to fulfil our requirements apart from God's will.

Determining Demons' Activities

Can we determine what demons are up to? We know that they are trying to influence and deceive us, but what exactly does that involve? We must identify how demons work in the world and how we can resist their efforts. One way to determine what demons are up to is to look at the Bible. The Bible contains stories about people who were influenced or deceived by demons. In Acts, there is a story about the man possessed by a demon. The demon made the man cry against Paul and Silas. In another story, a woman was possessed by a demon, which caused her to be crippled. Even after Paul prayed to her, the demon kept her from being healed.

To discern the activities of demons, it is important to observe their influence on individuals in contemporary society. Demons manifest their impact in diverse ways, leading people to experience negative thoughts, emotions, and behaviors. Their influence can extend to inciting individuals to engage in violent or harmful actions, thereby contributing to the perpetuation of discord and suffering. Moreover, demons are adept at deceiving individuals by instilling false beliefs and distorting their perceptions of reality. This deceitful influence can lead people astray, fostering misguided conviction and decisions. Hence, understanding the multifaceted ways in which demons influence human thoughts, behaviors, and beliefs is crucial for navigating the spiritual challenges present in the world today.

Demons Envy God's Creation

Demons envy God and His creation. Let us establish that demon hates everything about God and God's. First-way demons influence people by encouraging envy. The devil is jealous of God and His creation and tries to get us jealous so that we will not delight in what God has made. They desire to become enraged by individuals who possess what we lack, particularly when they are more righteous or spiritual than ourselves. As the serpent did with Eve in the Garden, they try to make us dissatisfied with our present lot and covet what is not ours, hoping that in the process, we will do something evil to gain or keep it (Gen 3:1-6).

Demons also propagate anger in the heart. In Matthew 5:22, Jesus warns against becoming angry at others without cause. Anger is a natural emotion, but it can easily lead to sin if it is not kept under control. We must always be careful about becoming angry for no reason or over petty matters, like someone taking a parking space from you or cutting in line ahead of us. These things should not bother us because we know that Jesus came to save us from hell, so why should a little earthly inconvenience matter? If you get angry about trivial things like this, your focus is on the things of this world rather than God's kingdom.

Jesus said that anger is like fire; if you do not control it, it can destroy you (Matt 5:22). Anger is a powerful emotion. An excellent example is illustrated in Genesis 4:3-5 when Cain became angry with Abel and murdered him. When Cain was asked about what happened to Abel, he lied about his whereabouts, saying that he did not even know where he was (vs. 9).

The point is that anger will cause us to sin, and then we will try to cover up that sin so that no one will know about it. So much for being honest!

It is typical for individuals who become enraged to experience more unpleasant repercussions than those with whom they are angry. Furthermore, by becoming angry about trivial matters, we may end up damaging relationships with others or creating bad experiences in our lives because of something we did while angry. Remember how Jonah got himself into trouble by becoming angry with God. He decided not to go where God sent him; instead, he got on a ship and sailed in the opposite direction, hoping to escape God's call in his life (Jonah 1).

When it comes to demons, one of the most important things to consider is their activities. This can be difficult because demons are often secretive and may not want to reveal their true nature. However, a number of indicators may provide insight into a demon's actions.

One of the first areas to begin is sin, associated with the demon. Demons are often related to sins such as lust, greed, and anger. Identifying the evil with which a demon is related can provide insights into the demon's intentions.

Another factor to consider is the type of damage caused by demons. Demons can cause physical harm such as injuries or property damage, but they can also cause emotional damage. If you see a demon causing emotional damage, such as terrorizing someone or forcing them to experience great fear, this is another clue regarding its activities. Finally, consider any other clues about the Demon's activities.

Demons Causes Temptation

Temptation is another major activity of demons. They tempt us with things we want or think we need, making us believe that we are not good enough, or will never be good enough. Temptation is a powerful tool that demons use. The Bible tells us that Satan tempted Jesus in the wilderness (Matthew 4:1-11).

This means that Jesus was not perfect, and he was tempted, just like we were. We must remember that it is not our fault when we are tempted; it is the work of demons trying to destroy us. When we are tempted, we need to pray for strength to resist, and ask God to help us see the temptation for what it really is.

The Bible tells us that demons possess people (Mark 5:1-20) This means that the devil controls the person's body and mind. The person is not in control of themselves. They may act differently than they usually do, and they may say things they would never say. They may do things they would never do. Possession is a serious matter that should be treated accordingly. Possession can happen to anyone, but is more likely to happen to weak people who have no faith in God. If you know someone possesses, you should pray for them and try to help them get help from a Christian counselor or pastor.

Demons Influencing Humans against God

When understanding demons and their activities, it is essential to realize that they are not all-powerful and are limited in what they can do by God's power. We can resist these attacks if we are prepared and have the right attitude.

One way to prepare ourselves is to study the Bible and learn about the spiritual armor God has provided for us. With this armor, we can stand against enemy schemes. Another way to prepare ourselves is to ask God to fill us with His Holy Spirit. When we are filled with Spirit, we will be better equipped to resist the enemy's temptations and attacks.

Another way to prepare is to build a relationship with God. When we are close to Him, His power works in us and through us. We can also ask Him for help when we feel attacked. If we are aware of the enemy's tactics and are prepared for the armor of God, we can resist his attacks. If you have never asked Jesus to be your Lord or Savior, now is the time to do so. Inviting Jesus into your life will give you the power you need to overcome the enemy.

Conclusion

Understanding the enemy is of utmost importance prior to undertaking the necessary planning and equipping ourselves for confrontation against evil forces ruled by the devil. In its boundless wisdom, God imparted to humanity His teachings on protecting oneself from the deceitful tactics employed by the devil. Acquiring a comprehensive understanding of the devil and his agents is instrumental in recognizing the strategies they employ to exert influence and profoundly impact our inner selves. It is commonly believed that demons primarily target external entities, often overlooking their profound impact on fundamental patterns of behavior. Understanding that the Lord's saints remain unaffected by the temptations and pernicious influences of the devil is of utmost importance. To overcome the wicked schemes of the devil, it is imperative that individuals engage in the process of unlearning this world and learning the coming world. The subsequent chapter explores strategies for actively participating in conflicts against malevolent forces. Now that we have effectively identified the subject in question, let us confront the evil entity and its associates to overcome their influence by appealing to Jesus.

Chapter 3

Defenders of the Faith: Uniting Against the Devil's Deception

> *"Be sober-minded; be watchful. Your adversary the devil prowls around like a roaring lion, seeking someone to devour. Resist him, firm in your faith, knowing that the same kinds of suffering are being experienced by your brotherhood throughout the world."*
>
> ***1 Peter 5:8-9***

In the realm of spirituality, the ongoing struggle between light and darkness remains constant. The character of the devil, as portrayed in Christian teachings, holds a prominent position as an embodiment of evil. This entity consistently works to subvert the righteous path and divert humanity away from the divine truth.

This chapter explores the determination of individuals who steadfastly serve as defenders of their religious beliefs, displaying unwavering dedication in their mission to counteract the devil's evil intentions. People from diverse cultural and religious backgrounds, unified by their shared Christian beliefs, often serve as emblems of hope in the face of deceptive situations.

In the context of Christian belief, the devil takes the role of tempter, enticing individuals who adhere to faith to deviate from the path of virtue using temptation and uncertainty. As we venture into the realm of darkness, we discover the power of unwavering faith and collective solidarity in overcoming the devil's deceitful charm and achieving victory.

Seizing the Initial Activities

The Bible tells us that we are not fighting the flesh and blood (Eph 6:12). It is a spiritual battle where our adversary is not just a demon; it is the kingdom of Satan and his demonic beings. We have much to do with spiritual warfare. The Bible teaches that, to be victorious, we must stand firm against him and resist temptations. In accordance with the teachings of scripture, it is imperative that we equip ourselves with the complete armor of God. We must begin with the question "How do I win my spiritual battle?" To achieve victory, we must persevere in our faith in God and resist the devil's temptation. Our unwavering trust in God serves as the initial line of defense in spiritual warfare.

The Devil also endeavors to mislead individuals by fostering the belief that their actions bear no repercussions. He may assert that they will evade detection or face no consequences in the event of engaging in wrong actions. This behavior may motivate individuals to engage in improper conduct or take part in actions that are considered morally unacceptable. The Devil also endeavors to foster discord and strife among the human population. One possible approach that he may employ involves creating an environment where individuals are motivated to engage in conflicts and disputes with one another. Alternatively, he may have endeavored to incite animosity and foster a climate of mutual suspicion among individuals.

The Devil frequently employs delusions and nightmares to manipulate individuals. He achieves this using visual representations of violence or suffering, which evoke feelings of fear and anxiety, resulting in emotional distress and psychological chaos. These disturbing ideas can deter individuals from pursuing ethical behavior or weaken their resolve to adhere to their beliefs.

On the other hand, it is conceivable that Satan could tempt people by offering them desirable images of comforting joy or captivating worldly pleasure. His intention behind this enticement is to encourage individuals to participate in immoral actions or give in to sinful desires, ultimately leading them away from divine standards.

Nonetheless, the previously mentioned illustration emphasizes the strategies individuals can employ to shield themselves against the evil influence of the Devil, specifically by adhering to the principles outlined in the Bible. The Bible guides ethical and spiritual teachings that function as a protective barrier against seductive temptations presented by the Devil. By following these teachings, individuals can bolster their faith and resist the deceitful charm of the devil's enticement.

Hence, it is imperative to maintain vigilance and awareness regarding the devil's evil plot. By being aware of his efforts to manipulate and deceive, individuals can enhance their readiness to counteract their allurements. This state of awareness encompasses the cognitive, affective, and behavioral dimensions of an individual while acknowledging the potential consequences of detrimental external factors. Let us explore the steps that are crucial to our initial approach to spiritual warfare.

The first step is to identify your Demons

Identifying your demons is like shining light on the shadows within yourself, and the Bible offers guidance on this transformative journey. Proverbs 4:23 advises, "Above all else, guard your heart, for everything you do flows from it." This underscores the importance of self-awareness and introspection as essential steps in recognizing personal challenges and conflicts. Journaling, as suggested in the scriptures, can be a powerful tool for delving into your internal realm, revealing recurring negative themes and patterns (Psalm 139:23-24).

Negativity often serves as a revealing sign of demonic influence, echoing the biblical warning in 1 Peter 5:8, "Be alert and of sober mind. Your enemy the devil prowls around like a roaring lion looking for someone to devour." Persistent negative thoughts and emotions can be an indicator of lurking demons. Similarly, Galatians 5:22-23 encourages identifying these influences by recognizing the fruits of the spirit, such as love, joy, peace, and self-control.

External influences, as mentioned in the Bible, can contribute to demonic manifestation (Ephesians 6:12). Evaluating relationships and surroundings aligns with biblical counseling to guard against detrimental influences. Psalm 26:2 urges, "Test me, Lord, and try me, examine my heart and my mind," emphasizing the importance of scrutinizing one's emotional state. Journaling is a way of documenting one's emotional states throughout the day with the aim of identifying patterns and triggers. The practice of journaling can be seen in Psalm 119:59, which states, "I thought about my ways, and turned my feet to Your testimonies." In this verse, Psalmist carefully examines his conduct and concludes that he has deviated from the path of God and the truth. By engaging in daily journaling, one can maintain a close connection with God and use this practice to strengthen their relationship with Him.

Patience is a virtue extolled in the Bible, and the process of self-identification is no exception (Galatians 6:9). Recognizing that this exploration can be complex and emotionally charged, scriptures counsel us to navigate with patience and empathy. The Bible also advocates for positive coping strategies and behaviors, echoing Philippians 4:8, "Finally, brothers and sisters, whatever is true, whatever is noble, whatever is right, whatever is pure, whatever is lovely, whatever is admirable—if anything is excellent or praiseworthy—think about such things."

Identifying demons is a crucial step, aligning with biblical wisdom, to be vigilant against negative influences. Seeking professional help through the Word of God becomes the recommended approach, acknowledging the transformative power of scriptural guidance in overcoming the influence of malevolent forces.

Planning is Essential

Strategic planning plays a pivotal role in achieving objectives and securing success; however, its importance cannot be emphasized. Establishing a carefully crafted plan is crucial for personal and professional pursuits as it provides a strong foundation for growth and success. Interestingly, even the devil employed strategic planning to execute its cunning schemes.

Understanding the methods and strategies employed by the devil can offer valuable insights into his attempts to lead people astray the righteous path. As a cunning deceiver, he actively seeks weaknesses and exploits them skillfully. Gaining knowledge of his tactics can help us fortify our defenses and safeguard ourselves and others from succumbing to his alluring temptation.

The devil tricks people by making tempting things appear appealing. He shows them attractive ideas that make them want to do things against what they believe is correct. These temptations may promise quick success, immediate pleasure, or fake happiness. However, it is crucial to understand that these ideas are illusions and, in the end, lead to feeling spiritually and morally empty. Imagine a student who is struggling with their studies and feeling the pressure to obtain good grades. The devil's strategy could involve creating deceptive temptation. Students might be tempted to cheat on the test, thinking that it is the easiest way to achieve a good grade and relieve stress instantly. The vision of success and promise of immediate relief from academic pressure may seem tempting. However, if students give in to this temptation, they will go against their personal values and principles of honesty and hard work. In the end, even if they obtain a good grade, they may experience a sense of spiritual and moral emptiness because they do not earn it through their own efforts and integrity. Let us consider another example of someone entering a relationship solely for physical pleasure without a genuine emotional connection. The devil's strategy might involve creating a deceptive manifestation of temptation by making the physical aspect appear overwhelmingly attractive. In this scenario, a person might be enticed by the promise of instant gratification and the illusion that physical pleasure alone can bring about lasting satisfaction. However, if they prioritize lustful desires over building a meaningful and respectful connection with their partner, they may eventually find themselves in a situation of emptiness and dissatisfaction, realizing that true fulfillment in a relationship involves more than just a physical attraction.

Furthermore, it is worth noting that the devil frequently exploits vulnerabilities and feelings of inadequacy. The devil may employ tactics, such as instilling fear, placing doubt, or highlighting previous mistakes to erode self-assurance and divert us from our intended course of action. The identification of these vulnerabilities grants individuals the ability to strengthen their defenses against assailants' actions, fostering the cultivation of resilience and steadfast resolutions. In instances of vulnerability, if not addressed through the intervention of God's power, the adversary exploits these frailties to wreak havoc on lives, fostering destructive outcomes, such as addiction, deepening states of depression, and tragically pushing individuals towards the perilous edge of suicide. The absence of spiritual resilience can render individuals more susceptible to the insidious influences of despair, leading them to a perilous path in which the destructive forces of addiction and mental health struggles can take a severe toll, ultimately posing a threat to their well-being. This underscores the importance of seeking spiritual guidance and support to face these challenging circumstances and prevent potential devastation that can be wrought by the evil forces that prey on vulnerability.

Knowing the signs that bad things might be around helps us see when we are in trouble. It is like a special sense that makes us more aware of the spiritual world. This awareness helps us to make the right choices and stay strong in what we believe. Consider the following example. Imagine you are hanging out with a new group of friends, and they start encouraging you to do something you know is wrong, such as stealing. If you have developed an understanding of the signs that suggest bad influences, you might notice feelings of discomfort. This could be your inner alarm, telling you that the situation is not good. This alarm can only be activated by the power of the Holy Spirit. It is triggered only when we engage in God's words and prayer.

With enhanced perception and awareness of the spiritual realm, one might decide to step back from that group and make a more informed choice. You could choose to stay true of your belief in honesty and avoid getting caught up in actions that could lead to trouble. In this way, being aware of indicators helps you make choices that align with your values and protects you from falling into situations influenced by dark forces. Success in reaching goals relies on having a plan, and this principle applies even to thwarting harmful intentions of the devil. Strategic planning is crucial in resisting and overcoming evil force schemes. By adopting a well-thought-out approach, individuals can better respond to the challenges posed by the devil and work towards their spiritual well-being. Enhancing our understanding of his tactics allows us to fortify our defenses against his ploys, thereby fostering an unshakable faith in God, dedication to moral principles, and self-improvement. By adhering to biblical core values and seeking spiritual guidance, we can shield ourselves from the deceptive tactics employed by evil forces and remain steadfast on a trajectory towards achievement and contentment.

A famous passage in the Old Testament offers a glimpse of how the devil plans. The Lord said to Satan, "Where have you come from?" Then Satan answered the Lord, saying, "From roaming about on the earth and walking around on it." And the Lord said to Satan, "Have you considered My servant Job? For there is no one like him on the earth, a blameless and upright man, fearing God and turning away from evil." Then Satan answered the Lord, "Does Job fear God for nothing? Have You not made a hedge about him and his house and all that he has on every side? You have blessed the work of his hands, and his possessions have increased in the land. But stretch out Your hand now and touch all that he has; he will surely curse You to Your face!" The Lord said to Satan, "Behold, all that he has is in your power; only do not put forth your hand on him!" So Satan went out from the presence of the Lord (Job 1:6-12).

Notice how this passage reveals Satan's plans. First, he dominates our planet by controlling and influencing people around it. He found Job and observed him. He subsequently formulated a plan to attack him. He does this by testing Job's faithfulness and bombarding him with trial and tribulation.

The devil always looks for people to be destroyed. He does this by tempting them into sin, leading them further down the path of destruction. We see this happening all the time around us. People start with minor sins and gradually move on to bigger and more destructive sins. The devil knows of our weaknesses and uses them against us.

We must be aware of and prepare for the devil's schemes. The best way to achieve this is to develop a close relationship with God. When we are walking with God, we are better able to resist the devil's temptation. We also need to be filled with the Holy Spirit to have the power to overcome enemy attacks.

The devil always looks for ways to destroy our lives and relationships with God. He does not attack us directly but instead uses deceit and manipulation to lure us into sin. We must always be on our guard and be aware of his schemes. Therefore, it is essential to plan.

Making a list of your weaknesses

The devil is constantly busy with his activities against humans to destroy them physically, mentally, and spiritually. In addition to his objective of annihilating God's creation, he maintains a keen view of humanity. What could be a more effective means of accomplishing this than cataloging vulnerabilities? Yes, I know what you're thinking: "The Devil is just trying to make us feel bad about ourselves." One of the devils' most effective tactics is to make us feel unimportant. He exploited this feeling to portray us as powerless and susceptible to harm, ultimately disrupting our relationship with God and undermining our sense of tranquility and unity.

Before the devil attacks us through our weaknesses, we must prayerfully list our shortcomings and spiritual challenges hindering our relationship with God.

1. *I am impatient.*
2. *I get angry quickly.*
3. *I am prideful.*

4. *I have a quick temper*
5. *I can be self-centered.*
6. *I can be critical of others.*
7. *I can be unforgiving.*
8. *I can have a judgmental attitude.*
9. *I can be resentful.*
10. *I can be jealous.*

Therefore, before the devil attacks us, we list our challenges and act on them. God simply desires to help us resist the devil and to improve our spiritual life. After all, if there is one thing I am confident about, humans always seek ways to improve themselves.

1. *I need to learn to be patient.*
2. *I need to learn to control my anger.*
3. *I need to learn to be humble.*
4. *I need to learn to forgive.*
5. *I need to learn to be tolerant of others.*
6. *I need to learn to be more positive.*
7. *I need to learn not to hold grudges.*
8. *I need to stop being so critical of others.*
9. *I need to work on letting go of my resentment.*
10. *I need to work on not being jealous.*

Initiating Countermeasures against the Devil

The ongoing conflict between good and evil has consistently intrigued human contemplation with the mystifying figure of the devil representing the epitome of wickedness. Through a thorough engagement investigating teaching in the Bible, we embark on a journey to unveil the subtle yet potent roots of the devil's malicious intent. By understanding these initial maneuvers, we can acquire valuable insights into the initiation of preventative measures to avert the potentially devastating consequences of their actions.

The devil always seeks to undermine the efforts to live a good and holy life. We must be vigilant about recognizing his devious schemes and acting against them. One way to do this is to be proactive in our spiritual lives. By concerted efforts to grow in our relationship with God, we make it more difficult for the devil to lure us away from His path. Furthermore, it is imperative that we exhibit diligence in passing the divine benevolence of God to our fellow humans through compassion, mercy, giving back, and guiding them on a path towards spiritual maturity. By engaging in such actions, we not only help individuals who need support but also create obstacles for evil forces to establish influence within our innermost beings.

Another way to fight the devil is to pray for those under his influence. During my early doctoral classes at Andrews University, my professor Dr. Bruce L. Bauer assigned an assignment that had a profound impact on me. The assignment was to pray to someone who was struggling under the influence of the devil. Since then, I have incorporated this practice into my teaching ministry at Spicer Adventist University, where I encourage my students to pray to one another. This activity has allowed me to witness firsthand the power of engaging with the devil and has been a valuable part of my almost decade-long teaching experience in the seminary. Every time we assigned this prayer, I heard heartwarming testimony from my students. By interceding on behalf of others, we help weaken the devil's hold over them and give them a better chance to resist his temptations. Finally, we should always be ready to offer encouragement and support to those struggling with the devil plots. In doing so, we not only provide them with much-needed assistance but also serve as a reminder that they are not alone in their fight.

Be Persistent

The Devil is always looking for ways to trip us up and discourage us from living a Christ-centered life. However, we can take the initiative and stay one step ahead by being persistent in our faith. In Ephesians 6:18, Paul says to "pray at all times in the Spirit, with all prayer and supplication. To that end keep alert with all perseverance, making supplication for all the saints." We must persist if we want to live a life that pleases God. We cannot allow ourselves to get complacent or take our eyes off from the prize. Instead, we must stay focused on Christ and ensure that our prayers are aligned with His will.

Christianity is not always easy to achieve. This can be tricky at times. However, this does not imply that we should abandon it. On the contrary, we need to press on and persevere through difficult times. In James 1:12, we are told that "Blessed is the one who perseveres under trial because, having stood the test, that person will receive the crown of life that the Lord has promised to those who love him." When we face trials and temptations, we must remember that God uses them to refine and make us more like Christ. Therefore, instead of giving up, we must trust that He knows what He is doing and keep our eyes on Him.

When it comes to living a Christ-centered life, there are many things we need to keep in mind. We must be aware of our motives, stay focused on Christ, and persist in faith. Most importantly, we must remember that God is under control. God knows what He is doing and will never leave or forsake us (Heb 13:5). So, even when things get hard or unclear, we must get back to God talking to Him through prayers and learn His guidance through the scriptures. In Luke 18:1, Jesus tells His disciples a parable of a widow who continually pestered a judge for justice. The judge eventually gave in, not because he cared about her case but because he was tired of her coming to him day after day (Lk 18:5). Jesus says that if an unrighteous judge can be worn down by persistence, how much more will our Heavenly Father answer our prayers when we cry out to Him?

When we take the lead, the devil can thwart our plans and hinder the progress. To achieve these goals, we must anticipate his schemes and defeat his strategies. He knows how to read people and what they want and is always ready to take advantage of an opportunity. Whether it is something as simple as offering someone a piece of candy or as complicated as tempting someone with power or money, the devil always looks for ways to get ahead. So, if you ever feel like you are behind in life, remember that the devil is always one step forward to attack—and therefore, be encouraged to be better and ahead to defeat him!

Engaging Spiritual Weapon

In a world filled with challenges and uncertainties, many people are in the quest to find spiritual understanding and a connection to something beyond themselves. As we go through the ups and downs of life, we often seek comfort and guidance to navigate through times of confusion and uncertainty. During this journey, God becomes a constant source of hope, providing timeless wisdom and divine insights to those who sincerely seek a path illuminated with light.

The quest for spiritual enlightenment and connection to God is a perennial and deeply ingrained pursuit. In the Bible, there are numerous verses that highlight the idea of seeking God for guidance and finding solace in His wisdom.

Jesus speaks about being a source of light and guidance in John 8:12, where he says, "I am the light of the world. Whoever follows me will never walk in darkness but will have the light of life." This reflects the concept that following God's path provides clarity and light amid life's uncertainty.

Therefore, the idea of seeking spiritual enlightenment and finding a connection with God is not just a modern pursuit; it has deep roots in the biblical context, where God is portrayed as a beacon of hope and wisdom for those navigating through the shadows of life.

The Bible serves as a repository of divine knowledge and moral teachings. It is a profound spiritual guide that illuminates the paths to salvation and righteousness. Within its pages, numerous passages and verses provide comfort, direction, and clarity to those grappling with the surrounding darkness. In Psalm 119:105, it is written, "Your word is a lamp to my feet and a light to my path." This powerful imagery highlights the transformative nature of God's word, portraying it as an illuminating force that dispels darkness and reveals the right course to follow. In times of confusion and distress, individuals can find guidance and assurance in these words, relying on God's wisdom to navigate their way through life challenges.

In addition, Jesus Christ's teachings offer profound insight into the nature of truth, love, and compassion. In John 8:12, Jesus declares, "I am the light of the world. Whoever follows me will not walk in darkness but will have the light of life." This declaration epitomizes the essence of spiritual seeking, embracing Christ's teachings as a source of divine illumination that leads believers away from the darkness of sin and towards the path of eternal life.

The Bible also emphasizes the significance of seeking divine guidance and wisdom through prayer. In James 1:5-6, it is written, "If any of you lacks wisdom, let him ask God, who gives generously to all without reproach, and it will be given him. But let him ask in faith, with no doubting, for the one who doubts is like a wave of the sea that is driven and tossed by the wind." This passage underscores the power of prayer as a means of seeking divine understanding and discernment. By approaching God with sincerity and faith, individuals can open themselves to receiving the spiritual insights necessary to discern the path of light amid the shadows of darkness.

Furthermore, Bible exhorts believers actively engage in a spiritual battle against darkness and evil. Ephesians 6:12 emphasizes, "For our struggle is not against flesh and blood, but against the rulers, against the authorities, against the powers of this dark world and against the spiritual forces of evil in the heavenly realms." This recognition of spiritual warfare underscores the necessity of wielding God as a spiritual weapon to combat evil force. By internalizing divine truths and teachings, individuals can equip themselves to resist temptation, overcome adversity, and spread the light of God's love to those around them. Embracing the teachings of Christ and engaging in earnest prayer, believers can wield the word 'God' as a transformative and empowering spiritual weapon, dispelling darkness, and illuminating the path towards a life of righteousness and eternal light. Let us briefly discuss the following questions.

What is the meaning of spiritual weapons?

In the spiritual realm, where battles are not fought with physical weapons but with intangible forces, the idea of spiritual weapons takes deep significance. Spiritual weapons are symbolic tools that people use to confront challenges and difficulties. Drawing from core biblical principles, these weapons offer strength, guidance, and protection on the journey towards inner peace and enlightenment. It is not about physicality but about embodying spiritual resilience.

In the Bible, we find the concepts of spiritual weapons in Ephesians 6:12, "For we do not wrestle against flesh and blood, but against principalities, against powers, against the rulers of the darkness of this age, against spiritual hosts of wickedness in the heavenly places." This text emphasizes the intangible nature of spiritual battles and the need for spiritual weapons. The arsenal of spiritual weapons must produce faith in God, prayerfulness, reading and learning the Bible, sharing love, showing compassion, practicing forgiveness, maintaining virtues and self-discipline. These elements come together as powerful forces that empower individuals in their spiritual journeys. By harnessing these spiritual forces, seekers discover their inner strengths, navigate challenges, and rise above darkness within themselves. As spiritual warriors, they emerge with a profound sense of purpose and deep understanding of the interconnectedness of all life. In this context, the true purpose of a spiritual weapon is to pave the way towards inner peace, enlightenment, and harmonious existence, aligning with the biblical principles of spiritual warfare and the tools needed for the journey.

Unlike physical weapons, a spiritual weapon is something that you use to defend yourself against negative energy or entities, instead of a weapon that you use to hurt or injure another person. For example, prayer is a form of communication between God and spiritual weapons (Mecca 2020). Through prayers, we engage our spiritual weapons to defend ourselves against adversaries. These spiritual weapons are not meant to be used against people but to safeguard us against negative energy or entities.

Effective utilization of spiritual weapons should manifest discernible outcomes. Conversely, if one fails to perceive or experience these results, they might be attributed to several factors, including inadequate preparation, an uncommitted spirit, and insufficient submission to the Holy Spirit. To overcome these challenges, one must persevere with faith and surrender to God to gain divine strength.

Here are some signs that your spiritual weapons are working.

1. You feel more positive and optimistic about your life.
2. You feel more in control of your own life and destiny.
3. You find it easier to connect with your spiritual side.
4. You have more clarity and focus on all aspects of your life.
5. You find yourself attracting more good life values.
6. Your relationships improve, attracting more supportive people into your life.
7. You feel a sense of protection from negative energy and do not get easily overwhelmed or bogged by stress.
8. You have more clarity about your life's purpose and what you need to do next.

What are the benefits of engaging in spiritual weapons?

As you read above, when you are equipped with spiritual weapons, you tap into a powerful source of energy and protection. Your spiritual weapons represent your highest self, and you are aligning yourself with God and engaging in unleashing His sovereignty. You can use your spiritual weapons to defend oneself and your loved ones from harm. Additionally, you can use it to help achieve your goals and success in your endeavors.

Engaging your spiritual weapon is an empowering experience that can help you connect with your insights and guidance. When you align with your highest purpose, you can draw on the unlimited reserves of power and protection. This can help to manifest your deepest desires, overcome challenges, and create a life you need to align with God while on earth.

When you engage with your spiritual weapon, you are open to a deeper connection with yourself and God. This can help you receive inner peace and clarity, gain strength and courage, and achieve life goals–above all, to prove allegiance with God.

How can your spiritual weapons be used effectively?

Although there is no written rule or standard procedure for using spiritual weapons, it is essential to use them effectively under God's guidance. There are a few suggestions to start and continue the practice effectively.

1. Explore spiritual weapons

Exploring spiritual weapons is a deeply personal and significant undertaking that can be approached through prayer, meditation, and self-reflection. It involves deliberate introspection into one's strengths, ideals, and attributes, considering the qualities that have proven effective in overcoming challenges or contributing to personal development. The importance of this exploration lies in its potential to uncover the innate resources that empower individuals on their spiritual journey.

By engaging in meditation or contemplation, visualizing oneself in challenging situations, and focusing on attributes that would aid in spiritual warfare, individuals can identify their spiritual weapons. Prayer is a central component, as it seeks divine guidance and clarity in cultivating specific qualities. This process is not only about personal reflection, but also about documenting insights through journaling, aligning with biblical principles that encourage the internalization of spiritual wisdom. Sharing this exploration with mentors, pastors, or a supportive community provides valuable insights and collective wisdom, reinforcing the biblical notion that spiritual growth is sharpened in the company of others (Pro 27:17).

Exploring spiritual weapons is a profound journey marked by prayer, meditation, and self-reflection, aimed at unveiling the intrinsic qualities that fortify individuals in their spiritual walk. It also involves meditation and contemplation, echoing the biblical wisdom found in Joshua 1:8, where it is proclaimed that meditating on God's law, day, and night brings success and prosperity. The Psalms, attributed to King David, also frequently emphasized the efficacy of meditation on God's words for spiritual strength and guidance.

Journaling, as a practice in this exploration, aligns with the biblical concept of writing God's commands on the tablet of one's heart (Pro 3:3-4). The act of documenting thoughts and insights serves as a tangible record of one's spiritual journey, thus facilitating growth and self-discovery.

Daily introspection is an effective and impactful practice that involves reflecting on one's life journey. By acknowledging God's guiding hand and taking a moment each day to appreciate it, individuals develop a deeper sense of gratitude. This ongoing awareness of God's presence, combined with an examination of the past and recognition of the divine direction in our lives, serves as a constant reminder of God's faithfulness. Engaging in this practice while exploring our daily experiences can foster a profound sense of thankfulness towards God for His unwavering guidance and grace, instilling a spirit of appreciation for the providence that has led us to the present moment.

Sharing our spiritual journey with close ones and family who are trustworthy and belong to a supportive community is based on the biblical principle of fellowship and mutual encouragement, as emphasized in Heb 10:24-25. The transformative impact of communal spiritual exploration stresses the mutual edification that occurs within a community of believers (Bonhoeffer 1954).

2. Use your spiritual weapon wisely

Imagine a scenario in which you find yourself facing a challenging situation—a colleague at work constantly undermines you, spreading rumors, and making your professional life difficult. At this moment of adversity, you have a choice: to retaliate with anger and hostility or to respond with wisdom and grace. This scenario reflects the battleground of spiritual warfare, where our actions and reactions can escalate conflicts or foster growth and reconciliation. As in this scenario, spiritual weapons play a crucial role in how we navigate life's challenges. From the shield of faith to the sword of the Spirit, these weapons empower us to overcome adversity and uphold God's truth. However, their effectiveness lies not only in their existence but also in how we wield them.

Effective utilization of spiritual weapons requires careful consideration and mindfulness. It is essential to use them wisely and understand their impact on oneself and others. For instance, if someone wrongs you and acts as an adversary, it resists the urge to retaliate with negative intention. Instead, channel your spiritual weapon towards personal growth and forgiveness, praying for transformation and reconciliation, as taught in Matthew 5:44: "But I tell you, love your enemies and pray for those who persecute you." Consider your intentions before employing spiritual weapons: are you seeking personal well-being, overcoming challenges, or contributing positively to spiritual growth? Clarity in your goals ensures constructive use.

Furthermore, we evaluated how your actions influenced those around you. A spiritual weapon should not cause harm, but inspire and uplift others, aligning with the purpose of God's people. As Ephesians 4:29 advises, "Do not let any unwholesome talk come out of your mouths, but only what is helpful for building others up according to their needs, that it may benefit those who listen." Focus on personal growth by refining and expanding the qualities of your spiritual weapon, allowing it to evolve alongside your development as a person.

Regularly assess the effectiveness of spiritual weapons and be open to adjustments if unintended consequences arise. Seek God's guidance in aligning your actions with His will and incorporating empathy and compassion into your approach. Understanding the perspectives and challenges of others enables one to foster understanding and connection, thus contributing to a harmonious spiritual journey. Practicing mindfulness in your actions ensures that your use of spiritual weapons remains consistent with your values and long-term goals, guiding you in the ongoing battle against forces of darkness.

3. Keep your spiritual weapons active and growing

Maintaining the effectiveness of spiritual weapons requires an open mind to receive new insights and methods from God's words and other sources. We must be willing to embrace change and challenge our assumptions by experimenting with various approaches to spiritual development. For instance, one student in our mentoring program confided in me about his fear of darkness and the shadows he saw. Upon further discussion, it became apparent that his exposure to horror movies and violent content fueled his anxiety. I encouraged him to refrain from watching such films, which led to significant improvement in his condition. However, the root cause of his desire for scary entertainment is his social circle. Through ongoing support and guidance, he gradually distanced himself from friends who negatively influenced his choice. Over time, he has experienced a profound transformation in his spiritual life through prayer, scripture reading, and regular church attendance.

Reflecting on past experiences helps us discern what strategies have been effective and what adjustments are required for future growth. Seeking guidance from mentors and like-minded individuals provides valuable perspectives and support for refining spiritual practices. Regular contemplation allowed us to evaluate the impact of spiritual weapons and identify areas for improvement. It is essential to recognize that the effectiveness of these tools may vary depending on the situation, requiring adaptability while upholding the core principles.

Drawing from God's word, Proverbs 15:22 reminds us, "Plans fail for lack of counsel, but with many advisers they succeed." This underscores the importance of seeking counsel from others on our spiritual journey. Similarly, James 1:5 encourages us to seek wisdom from God, promising that He will generously provide guidance to those asking.

Nurturing spiritual growth involves the continuous process of exploration, reflection, and adaptation. By remaining open to new revelations, learning from past experiences, and seeking support from mentors and peers, we can effectively wield spiritual weapons and experience transformative growth in our relationship with God.

4. Be aware of your spiritual weapons throughout the day

Imagine a busy day at work. You rush from one meeting to the next, with a to-do list that seems to grow longer by the minute. Amidst chaos, you receive a phone call with news that throws you off balance—a project deadline moved up, a conflict with a colleague, or perhaps a personal challenge weighing heavily on your mind. In such moments, it is easy to feel overwhelmed and lost. However, what if, amid chaos, you had a reliable source of strength and guidance? What if you could tap into a reservoir of inner peace and resilience that helped you navigate challenges with grace and wisdom? This is where the concept of spiritual weapons comes into play—a set of tools and practices that empower individuals to face life is a challenge with courage and faith—only when we are constantly aware of spiritual weapons.

Being aware of our spiritual weapons is crucial for their effective use and for avoiding unintentional neglect. Setting reminders on our devices can help prompt us to pause and reflect regularly on our spiritual weapons. As Proverbs 3:6 advises, "In all your ways acknowledge him, and he will make straight your paths." This acknowledgment includes moments of prayer, Bible reading, or simply reflecting on God's presence in our lives.

Personally, I integrated this practice into my daily routine by setting five alarms on my phone to ring at different times throughout the day. This is not about adhering to any specific religious practice but about acknowledging God's presence and grace in my life. Taking these moments to contemplate His goodness and my own unworthiness has been humbling and motivating. It is a simple yet powerful confession that helps me realign my focus and renew my commitment to serving Him.

Mindfulness exercises also play a role in incorporating spiritual weapons into daily life. By taking a few moments to center ourselves in the present, we can intentionally connect with our spiritual weapons and cultivate gratitude for their influence. This gratitude, as expressed in Colossians 3:17, reminds us to "do everything in the name of the Lord Jesus, giving thanks to God the Father through him."

Furthermore, engaging in regular self-reflection throughout the day can help gauge the effectiveness of using spiritual weapons. Asking ourselves questions like, "Am I using my spiritual weapon effectively in this situation?" allows for ongoing self-assessment and course corrections. This self-check-in, inspired by passages like 2 Corinthians 13:5 "Examine yourselves to see whether you are in the faith; test yourselves. Do you not realize that Christ Jesus is in you—unless, of course, you fail the test?" that encourages self-examination, keeps us aligned with our spiritual goals, and fosters continuous growth and transformation in our faith journey.

5. Stay positive and maintain a positive attitude

In the heart of a bustling city, amidst concrete and steel lies a small community garden tended by a dedicated gardener named Lily. Despite the challenges of urban life, Lily's Garden serves as an oasis for tranquility and beauty. Each morning, as the sun rises over the skyline, Lily emerges with her watering can and trowel ready to nurture her beloved plants. One day, a storm sweeps through the city, bringing torrential rain and strong wind. The garden is battered, with uprooted plants and flowers wilting under the weight of the downpour. However, amidst chaos, Lily remains undeterred. With unwavering optimism, she begins the work of restoration, gently replanting the fallen seedlings and tending to the bruised blooms. As days pass, the garden begins to recover, bursting with a new life and color. Lily's positive attitude and steadfast dedication transformed the once-damaged garden into a flourishing haven of hope and resilience, reminding everyone who passed by the power of optimism in the face of adversity.

Maintaining a positive attitude is vital when wielding spiritual weapons, much like Lily's unwavering optimism amid the storm. Just as negativity can hinder effectiveness, a cheerful mindset can empower their impact. Philippians 4:8 advise us to focus on whatever is true, noble, right, pure, lovely, and admirable, highlighting the importance of a positive outlook in spiritual warfare.

Regularly reminding ourselves of our blessings shifts our focus away from negativity and towards gratitude, as Psalm 103:2 encourages us to "Praise the Lord, my soul, and forget not all his benefits." Counting our blessings cultivates a thankful heart and strengthens our spiritual resilience.

Positive affirmations aligned with the characteristics of our spiritual weapons can reinforce an optimistic mindset, echoing the wisdom of Proverbs 18:21 that "The tongue has the power of life and death." Speaking positive words over our lives affirms our faith and empowers our spiritual journeys.

The mindfulness of our thoughts and emotions allows us to acknowledge negative feelings without succumbing to them, as Philippians 4:6-7 teaches us to present our requests to God with thanksgiving, resulting in peace that transcends our understanding. By focusing on positive aspects, we invite God's peace into our hearts and situations.

Visualizing positive outcomes and scenarios while wielding spiritual weapons enhances their effectiveness, as Proverbs 23:7 reminds us that "For as he thinks in his heart, so is he." Our thoughts shape our reality, and envisioning positive outcomes aligns our actions with God's plans for us.

Treating ourselves with compassion and love, especially in difficult circumstances, reflects the biblical principle of loving others as ourselves (Mark 12:31). Recognizing our imperfections and viewing setbacks as opportunities for growth echoes Romans 8:28, assuring us that God works for the good of those who love Him.

Maintaining an optimistic attitude fosters innovative problem-solving and action, as encouraged by James 1:2-4, which urges believers to consider trials as opportunities for perseverance and maturity. Surrounded by positive influences and cultivating empathy for ourselves and others, we can embrace positivity and thrive on our spiritual journey.

Staying positive while wielding spiritual weapons involves nurturing a mindset of gratitude, affirmation, mindfulness, and resilience rooted in biblical principles. By embracing positivity, we can overcome obstacles and flourish in our spiritual growth, much like Lily's Garden blooming amidst storms of life.

6. Be grateful for your spiritual weapon

Imagine a skilled archer who, after years of practice, receives a finely crafted bow and arrow set as a gift. Grateful of this new tool that enhances their abilities, they express thanks to the giver and eagerly begin honing their skills with it. Similarly, in our spiritual journey, we are equipped with spiritual weapons by God to navigate life's challenges and to grow as individuals. Just as the archer appreciates their new bow, we must be grateful for our spiritual weapons and their roles in our personal development.

Reflecting on Psalm 144:1, "Praise be to the Lord my Rock, who trains my hands for war, my fingers for battle," we see how God equips us with the necessary tools for spiritual warfare. Expressing gratitude for these weapons acknowledges God's provision and empowers us to effectively wield them.

Taking time each day to contemplate our spiritual weapons and the positive traits they represent fosters gratitude and mindfulness. We can thank God for the strength of faith, the shield of righteousness, the sword of the Spirit, and other spiritual tools that guide us in our journey. Philippians 4:6-7 encourages us to "present [our] requests to God," indicating the importance of expressing gratitude for His assistance in navigating challenges and promoting personal growth.

During meditation, we can focus on spiritual weapons and envision them as sources of strength and guidance. As we visualize these qualities, directing us towards positive outcomes, we cultivate a deep sense of gratitude for their presence in our lives. This gratitude not only enhances our spiritual well-being but also empowers us to face life trials with confidence and resilience. Through thankfulness for our spiritual weapons, we acknowledge God's blessings and invite His continued guidance and provision in our lives.

7. Be open to feedback

Being open to feedback is crucial in honing spiritual weapons for effective use in our journey. Just as a blacksmith refines a sword through external inputs, we can also benefit from the insights and observations of others. Proverbs 15:22 advises, "Plans fail for lack of counsel, but with many advisers they succeed." This biblical principle underscores the importance of seeking feedback from others for spiritual growth.

When we use our spiritual weapons, whether it is prayer, scripture reading, or acts of kindness, feedback from fellow believers can provide valuable insights into their effectiveness. Psalm 141:5 says, "Let a righteous man strike me—that is kindness; let him rebuke me—that is oil on my head. My head will not refuse it, for my prayer will still be against the deeds of evildoers." This verse emphasizes the humility required to accept feedback and the benefits it brings to our spiritual journeys.

Moreover, being open to feedback allows us to recognize that our spiritual weapons require adjustment. Just as a sword may dull over time and require sharpening, spiritual practices may lose their effectiveness if not adapted to changing circumstances. By embracing feedback and being willing to experiment using different approaches, we can refine our spiritual arsenal for continued growth and effectiveness.

Hence, being open to feedback is vital to spiritual growth. By seeking input from others, we gain valuable perspectives on our spiritual journey and the effectiveness of spiritual weapons. Through humility and openness, we can refine our practices, ensuring that they remain sharp and effective in the battles we face.

Engaging with the Bible

Engaging with the Bible is not merely about passive reading or intellectual understanding; it is about actively involving ourselves in God's words, just as Jesus and countless others have done throughout the Bible. In Matthew 4:1-11, Jesus combated the temptations of the devil by quoting Scripture, demonstrating the power of engaging with God's words in spiritual warfare. Likewise, in Daniel 1:8, Daniel resolved not to defile himself with the king's food, choosing instead to align his actions with God's command. These examples highlight the proactive approach to spiritual life encouraged by the Bible.

Engaging with the Bible means taking charge of our spiritual lives and actively seeking God's guidance and wisdom in every aspect. It involves proactive steps in our daily routine and applying biblical principles to decisions and actions. Just as athletes train diligently to excel in their sport, we must train ourselves spiritually by immersing ourselves in the Word of God and allowing it to shape our thoughts, attitudes, and behaviors.

Moreover, engaging with the Bible entails taking risks for the sake of the gospel and stepping out of our comfort zones to share the message of God's love and salvation with others. We put ourselves in situations where we will be stretched and challenged spiritually (One, 2019). Acts 4:29-31 illustrate this boldness, as the early disciples prayed for courage to proclaim the gospel in the face of opposition. Similarly, we are called upon to proclaim the truth fearlessly and trust God's strength and presence. And we do all this knowing that God is with us and will never leave us alone. So, what specific ways can we take initiative in our spiritual lives?

1. Pray regularly and consistently. Regular and consistent prayers are powerful tools for our spiritual arsenal (Wagner 1997, 16). Through prayer, we engage in conversations with God, seeking direction and an understanding of our lives. As Jesus instructs in Matthew 6:6, "But when you pray, go into your room, close the door and pray to your Father, who is unseen. Then your Father, who sees what is done in secret, will reward you." This intimate communication with God strengthens our relationship with Him and empowers us to navigate through life challenges.

2. Read the Bible daily. Daily reading of the Bible is essential for deepening our connection with God and aligning ourselves with His will (Hughes 2013, 31). As we immerse ourselves in scripture, we gain insight into God's character and His intended path to our lives. Psalm 119:105

affirms the illuminating power of God's word: "Your word is a lamp for my feet, a light on my path." By investing time in studying the Bible, we equip ourselves with the wisdom and guidance required to live according to God's principles.

3. Serve others. Serving others is a tangible expression of faith and love for God (Matthew 25:40). Engaging in acts of service not only reflects the teachings of the Bible, but also spreads the love of Christ to those in need. By following Jesus' example of humility and selflessness, we demonstrate His compassion and its positive impact on our communities.

4. Share your faith. This is probably the most challenging task on this list, but it is also one of the most important. Sharing our faith with others is a crucial aspect of fulfilling the Great Commission (Matthew 28:19-20). Proclaiming the gospel opens the door for others to know Christ and experience His transformative love. As believers, we are called ambassadors to Christ, sharing His message of salvation with boldness and conviction.

5. Seek God first. Prioritizing God above all else is paramount in our spiritual journey (Matthew 6:33). By seeking God first and foremost, we align ourselves with His divine plans and purposes for our lives. Placing God at the center of our thoughts, decisions, and actions ensures that we remain grounded in His Truth and obey His will.

6. Be prepared mentally and emotionally. To effectively engage in spiritual warfare, mental and emotional preparation is crucial. This entails understanding the tactics of the enemy and their ability to withstand them. The Bible provides invaluable insights into the devil's strategies, alerting us to his snares and methods of deception. Through biblical engagement, we become aware of both active and passive forms of demonic influence, empowering us to prepare ourselves mentally and emotionally for the spiritual battle ahead. Ephesians 6:11 encourages believers to "put on the full armor of God so that you can take your stand against the devil's schemes."

7. Be bold and courageous. Immersing ourselves in the Bible equips us with boldness and courage. With a deep understanding of God's promises and sovereignty, we can fearlessly approach spiritual warfare. Rather than cowering in fear, we are encouraged to boldly wield our spiritual weapons, knowing that no power is greater than that of God. Joshua 1:9 assures us, "Be strong and courageous. Do not be afraid; do not be discouraged, for the Lord your God will be with you wherever you go."

8. Use your spiritual weapon wisely. Immersing ourselves in the Bible equips us with boldness and courage. With a deep understanding of God's promises and sovereignty, we can fearlessly approach spiritual warfare. Rather than cowering in fear, we are encouraged to boldly wield our spiritual weapons, knowing that no power is greater than that of God. Joshua 1:9 assures us, "Be strong and courageous. Do not be afraid; do not be discouraged, for the Lord your God will be with you wherever you go."

These are just a few simple steps to be remembered and to get you started. The most important thing is to be humble and to do whatever one can stay close to God. He will bless us for our efforts, and we will never regret taking initiative in our spiritual life. It is up to us to find ways to engage in spiritual weapons. Ultimately, our goal should be to connect with God.

The Word of God serves as a guide, teaching us how to use these weapons effectively for the advancement of God's kingdom and the defeat of spiritual adversaries. By remaining humble and steadfast in our pursuit of God, we invite His blessings and guidance into our lives, ensuring that our efforts to take the initiative in our spiritual journey are met with divine favor and fulfillment.

Conclusion

In our journey through the spiritual battlefield, we have uncovered the ever-present struggle between light and darkness, embodied in the adversary, the devil. The devil's role as a deceiver and tempter is a constant threat, aiming to lure believers away from the righteous path and into a life of sin and despair. Yet, the power of unwavering faith and the strength found in collective solidarity provide a formidable defense against these dark forces. In this chapter, we explored the determination and resilience of those who stand as defenders of their faith, united by their shared beliefs and commitment to countering the devil's malevolent schemes. These individuals, drawn from diverse cultural and religious backgrounds, serve as beacons of hope and exemplify the victory that can be achieved through steadfast faith and unity.

Chapter 4

Do Not Forget the Armor of God

"Do not forget the Armor of God, for it is your strength and protection in the battle against darkness."
Ephesians 6:11

In the Bible, the armor of God serves as spiritual protection. It is a reminder that, when we encounter spiritual dangers, we must clothe ourselves with God's armor. Amidst life's challenges, it is easy to forget that we have a divine protector who will guide us through every trial. God equipped us with His armor to combat the devil's schemes and thwart his evil plans. This armor includes the power of God's spirit, the shield of faith, and the assurance of salvation. When we have God's armor, we find shelter from the assault of the devil. Even in the face of adversity, we can walk in faith knowing that our salvation acts as a shield to withstand all forms of evil. With God, we can navigate through every difficulty with confidence and assurance.

The Devil and his Tricks

Once, a woman is distressed about her marriage. Feeling lost, she visits the fortuneteller to seek advice. The fortuneteller predicted that she would marry within a year but warned her to avoid her in-laws for a successful marriage. Trusting these words, she moved in with her husband and steered clear of her in-laws. However, her husband felt hurt by the division and disrespect toward his family. Their bond weakened, leading to a divorce two years later. Despite her efforts, the path she chose did not lead to the happy ending she hoped for.

Another anecdote is given about the pastor of a Christian church whose daughter was suffering from terminal disease. After seeking all the available medical options, he was left with no hope that his child would survive. Ultimately, the pastor sought the advice of a witch doctor who predicted that the child would not survive until the following day. The child of the pastor passed the next day.

In the world we live in today, there are many distractions and voices all around us, each trying to grab our attention. They promise quick fixes and easy solutions that seem tempting. Sometimes, we are drawn to these ideas because they promise immediate benefits, even though they might not be the best for us in the long run.

Our own desires for things, such as happiness and success, can sometimes lead us astray. We might believe what we want to hear rather than what is truly right, as taught by God. It is in these moments of vulnerability that we can be misled, taking us away from the solid teachings and guidance God offers.

The devil always looks for a way in and uses these moments to trick us. By spreading lies and illusions, he tries to draw us away from the comforting love of God, the protective shield of His care, and the haven found in His grace. Through clever tactics and false promises, the devil tries to pull us towards paths that deviate from the good ways of God, separating us from the comforting presence of divine love.

It is like a delicate dance we are in, balancing the potential benefits of shortcuts against the enduring truths God teaches us. To stay strong against the devil's schemes and remain anchored in God's love, we must faithfully follow His teachings. By choosing the path lit up by our faith, we can resist deceptions and stand firm in the warmth of God's love and unfailing protection.

The devil's ability to offer a morally and spiritually corrupt compromise is one of the most devious tricks he possesses. He knows that he cannot directly confront experienced believers with an attack on their morals and beliefs, and so he avoids doing so. Because we need to discern lies, we must continue to meditate on His words. When we realize that the devil has tricked us, we have the responsibility to seek accountability and repent our sins swiftly. Those who want to live lives that are pleasing to God should take comfort in the words of Psalm 37:23–24, that say, "The feet of a man are determined by the LORD when he delights in his way; if he falls, he shall not be flung headlong, for the LORD upholds his hand." When the Lord is on our side, the devil's tricks have no effect.

You must heed what God is trying to communicate to you to find direction in your life. If you obey His divine directions, He will assist you in accomplishing all that you set out to do, because He knows what is best for you.

Analyze the Enemy's Weaknesses

The first step in defeating an enemy is understanding them. It is crucial to study their existence, activities, and impact. When you know what makes them vulnerable, you can use them wisely. In a more straightforward manner, the devil's weakness is anything and everything that is of God. When enemies feel undervalued or unsupported, they are likely to feel weak. The devil loses confidence when he does not receive support in sin or wrongdoing. Afterwards, he feeds on our sins. Therefore, understanding the weaknesses of a devil can lead to success in any spiritual battle.

Exploiting the Weakness of the Enemy

To achieve success in any of the world's competitive activities, it is crucial to understand opponents' shortcomings. The same principle applies here, allowing you to profit from competitors' errors and surpass them by recognizing their vulnerabilities. Similar to how opponents make mistakes that can be utilized to achieve victory in life, in the same manner, in our spiritual life, we acknowledge that our conflict is against evil and triumph is difficult to attain unless we are knowledgeable about our adversary's weaknesses.

The Bible advises us that our adversary is Satan (Rev 12:9); thus, it is vital to recognize his vulnerabilities. Despite being a powerful spirit, Satan has fallen from heaven and into the eyes of God (Isa 14:12), which implies that he possesses certain limitations. Identifying his weaknesses is critical to spiritual warfare. By targeting his vulnerabilities, we can empower ourselves to resist his evil plots. Being aware of his strengths and weaknesses helps us better prepare for the battle. Although the devil is powerful in many ways, he is also weak in several areas. To effectively strategize against him, it is crucial to target his weaknesses. By understanding what makes him vulnerable, we can take advantage of his weaknesses and defeat him easily.

He cannot withstand God's wrath, as revealed in Revelation 20:10, and will ultimately rebel against Him, according to 2 Thessalonians 2:3-8. Similarly, we can identify Satan's weaknesses in our lives. He desires for us to be enslaved to sin, as per Hebrews 2:14, but we can resist him by adhering to the teachings of Jesus Christ, as mentioned in John 8:31-32.

The Armor of God

The concept of the "Armor of God" is deeply rooted in biblical teachings, serving as a powerful metaphor for the spiritual protection and readiness that believers must embrace to overcome the challenges of life and combat spiritual warfare. Ephesians 6:10-18 provides a vivid illustration of this spiritual armor, emphasizing its importance in equipping Christians to withstand the schemes of the enemy. In examining each component of this spiritual armor, we uncover profound insights into the importance of truth, righteousness, peace, faith, salvation, and the Word of God in our spiritual journey. Through a comprehensive understanding of the armor of God, we are empowered to stand firm in our faith, resist temptation, and emerge victorious in spiritual battles. Thus, let us embark on a journey to explore the depth of this spiritual armor and uncover its timeless relevance for believers today.

1. ***Belt of truth (Ephesians 6:14)***: The belt of truth serves as the foundational piece of spiritual armor, holding everything together in the life of a believer. This essential piece symbolizes the importance of living in alignment with God's truth and the integrity it brings to one's spiritual journey. Just as a physical belt secures a soldier's armor and enables them to move freely, the belt of truth enables believers to stand firm in their faith and cross through life challenges with confidence and conviction.

   Ephesians 6:14 highlights the significance of the belt of truth, urging believers to "stand firm then, with the belt of truth buckled around your waist." This imagery emphasizes the necessity of truthfulness and sincerity in the lives of Christians. By embracing God's truth and allowing it to permeate every aspect of their being, believers can anchor themselves securely in their faith and withstand enemy attacks.

   Living in accordance with God's truth involves more than just knowing the facts; it requires commitment to righteousness and honesty in all aspects of life. Proverbs 3:3-4 emphasizes the importance of embracing truth and living with integrity, stating, "Let love and faithfulness never leave you; bind them around your neck, write them on the tablet of your heart. Then you will win favor and a good name in the sight of God and man." This passage underscores the transformative power of truth and its ability to bring blessings and favor from God.

   Furthermore, the belt of truth serves as a defence against the deceitful schemes of the enemy. 1 Peter 5:8 warns believers to "be alert and of sober mind. Your enemy the devil prowls around like a roaring lion looking for someone to devour." In a world filled with falsehoods and deception, it is essential for believers to remain grounded in God's truth and discern lies propagated by the enemy.

   As believers clothe themselves with the belt of truth, they not only fortify their own spiritual foundation, but also become beacons of light and truth in a dark and deceptive world. By embodying the principles of honesty, integrity, and righteousness, believers can stand firm in their faith and fulfill their calling as ambassadors of Christ. Thus, the belt of truth serves as a vital component of the believer's spiritual armor, enabling them to walk in light of God's truth and withstand the attacks of the enemy.

2. ***Breastplate of righteousness (Ephesians 6:14)*****:** The breastplate of righteousness is a vital component of spiritual armor, serving as a protective shield for the heart and symbolizing moral purity and uprightness in the life of a believer. Just as a physical breastplate guards a soldier's vital organs in battle, the breastplate of righteousness safeguards the believer's spiritual heart from attacks by the enemy aimed at corrupting their character and integrity.

   The concept of righteousness is deeply rooted in scripture, emphasizing the importance of living in alignment with God's moral standards and command. In Psalm 119:172, it states, "May my tongue sing of your word, for all your commands are righteous." This verse underscores the righteousness inherent in God's commands, serving as a guide for believers to walk in righteousness.

   Furthermore, the New Testament emphasizes the significance of righteousness as a characteristic in the life of a believer. In Matthew 5:6, Jesus declares, "Blessed are those who hunger and thirst for righteousness, for they will be filled." This verse highlights the pursuit of righteousness as a foundational aspect of the Christian faith, leading to spiritual fulfillment and satisfaction. Unlike the unkind, ruthless world, believers in Christ are seen as righteous saints of God. Such a character is unseen among others, reflecting our allegiance to God.

   The breastplate of righteousness not only protects the believer's heart from being diluted but also serves as a testament to their commitment to live according to God's standards. In Romans

6:13, believers are urged, "Do not offer any part of yourself to sin as an instrument of wickedness, but rather offer yourselves to God as those who have been brought from death to life; and offer every part of yourself to him as an instrument of righteousness." This verse emphasizes the believer's

responsibility to actively pursue righteousness and reject sin.

Moreover, the breastplate of righteousness enables believers to withstand enemy attacks by standing firm in their convictions and moral integrity. In Ephesians 6:14, believers are exhorted to "stand firm then, with the belt of truth buckled around your waist, with the breastplate of righteousness in place." This verse emphasizes the importance of righteousness as a foundational aspect of a believer's spiritual armor, providing protection against spiritual attacks.

The breastplate of righteousness serves as a crucial piece of spiritual armor, guarding the believer's heart and integrity against the schemes of the enemy. Believers can stand firm in their faith and withstand the challenges of spiritual warfare through the pursuit of righteousness and obedience to God's commands.

3. ***Shoes of the Gospel of Peace (Ephesians 6:15)*:** The Shoes of the Gospel of Peace represent readiness and firm footing in sharing the message of salvation with others. Just as shoes provide stability and mobility for soldiers, the gospel equips believers to stand firm in their faith and journey confidently in spreading God's peace to the world.

   One of the foundational aspects of Christianity is the need to share good news with others. In Matthew 28:19-20, known as the Great Commission, Jesus instructs his disciples to "go and make disciples of all nations, baptizing them in the name of the Father and of the Son and of the Holy Spirit, and teaching them to obey everything I have commanded you." This command extends to all believers, urging them to proclaim the gospel and to bring others into a relationship with Christ.

The shoes of the gospel of peace also signify the importance of readiness and preparedness for evangelism. In 1 Peter 3:15, believers are encouraged to "always be prepared to give an answer to everyone who asks you to give the reason for the hope that you have." Readiness requires a deep understanding of the gospel message and the willingness to share it with boldness and clarity.

Furthermore, the shoes of the gospel of peace remind believers of the transformative power of God's peace in their lives. In John 14:27, Jesus declares, "Peace I leave with you; my peace I give you. I do not give to you as the world gives. Do not let your hearts be troubled and do not be afraid." This peace, which surpasses all understanding, not only guards our hearts and minds (Phil 4:7), but also serves as a testimony to others of the transformative work of Christ in our lives.

As believers journey through life, the shoes of the gospel of peace enable them to walk confidently in their faith, spreading God's peace to a broken and hurting world. By being rooted in the gospel message and living lives that reflect the peace of Christ, believers become powerful witnesses of God's love and grace toward those around them.

4. ***Shield of faith (Ephesians 6:16).*** The shield of faith is a critical component of a believer's spiritual armor, serving as a defensive weapon against the enemy's attacks of doubt and fear. It is essential to understand that this faith is not something innate within us but a precious gift bestowed upon us by God Himself. As Romans 12:3 affirms, "For by the grace given me I say to every one of you: Do not think of yourself more highly than you ought, but rather think of yourself with sober judgment, in accordance with the faith God has distributed to each of you." This verse highlights

that God has graciously given each believer a measure of faith, empowering them to stand firm against the adversary's assaults.

As believers walk with God and cultivate their relationship with Him, their faith grows and matures, becoming a shield that protects them from the fiery darts of the enemy. Just as physical shields provide cover and defense in times of battle, our faith serves as a shield that guards our hearts and minds against assaults of doubt and fear. Ephesians 6:16 urges believers to "take up the shield of faith, with which you can extinguish all the flaming arrows of the evil one." This verse underscores the defensive power of faith in spiritual warfare, emphasizing that it has the capability to extinguish every fiery dart launched by the enemy.

Furthermore, our faith not only serves as a defensive shield, but also enables us to live victorious lives in Christ. Hebrews 11:1 defines faith as "confidence in what we hope for and assurance about what we do not see." This assurance empowers believers to overcome obstacles and challenges, trust God's promises, and His faithfulness. As we exercise faith in God's Word and His promises, we can navigate through life's trials with confidence and assurance, knowing that our trust in Him will ultimately lead to victory.

Hence, the shield of faith is a vital component of the believer's spiritual armor, providing protection against enemy attacks and enabling us to live victorious lives in Christ. As we walk with God and nurture our relationships with Him, our faith grows and strengthens, serving as a powerful shield that guards our hearts and minds. Through faith, we can extinguish the fiery arrows of doubt and fear, trusting God's promises, and His faithfulness to lead us to triumph.

5. ***Helmet of Salvation (Ephesians 6:17).*** The Helmet of Salvation serves as a crucial piece of spiritual armor, safeguarding the believer's mind and thoughts. In Ephesians 6:17, believers are instructed to take up the helmet of salvation, emphasizing its

significance in spiritual warfare. Just as a physical helmet protects the head, the helmet of salvation shields the believer's mind from doubts, fears, and spiritual attacks.

The head is considered the most vital part of the body as it is the seat of thought and intellect. Therefore, protecting the mind is essential to maintaining spiritual strength and clarity. When we firmly grasp the assurance of our salvation in Christ, we find peace that transcends worldly disturbance. Romans 8:38-39 reassures believers of the unshakable security they have in Christ: "For I am convinced that neither death nor life, neither angels nor demons, neither the present nor the future, nor any powers, neither height nor depth, nor anything else in all creation, will be able to separate us from the love of God that is in Christ Jesus our Lord."

The helmet of salvation also serves as a reminder of the forgiveness of sins and the redemption offered through Christ's sacrifices. When we anchor our identity to Christ and acknowledge the forgiveness of our sins, we experience a deep sense of peace and security. Colossians 3:1-2 encourage believers to set their minds on things above, where Christ is seated at the right hand of God, reinforcing the importance of aligning our thoughts with the truth of salvation.

In times of spiritual warfare and uncertainty, the helmet of salvation serves as a steadfast anchor for a believer's mind. By embracing the assurance of salvation and dwelling on the truth of God's Word, we can overcome doubt and fear, standing firm in faith. Philippians 4:7 promises, "And the peace of God, which transcends all understanding, will guard your hearts and your minds in Christ Jesus," highlighting the profound peace that comes from knowing and embracing the salvation found in Christ.

6. ***Sword of spirit (Ephesians 6:17).*** The Sword of the Spirit, as described in Ephesians 6:17, stands out as the sole offensive weapon in God's armor. While other pieces primarily serve

defensive purposes, the sword of the Spirit empowers believers to actively engage in spiritual warfare. This weapon is none other than the Bible itself, often referred to as "living and powerful, sharper than any two-edged sword" (Heb 4:12). Just as a physical sword is wielded in battle, the Word of God serves as a potent tool for believers to combat enemy schemes.

When confronted by Satan during His time in the wilderness, Jesus exemplified the effective use of the sword of the Spirit. In each temptation, He countered the truth of scripture, demonstrating the power of God's word to overcome the adversary. Similarly, King David acknowledged the illuminating guidance provided by God's Word, declaring, "Your word is a lamp to my feet and a light to my path" (Ps 119:105). This imagery emphasizes the transformative and guiding nature of scripture in navigating life's challenges and staying on a path of righteousness.

The sword of God's Word serves a dual purpose: it defends believers against attacks by the enemy, while simultaneously dismantling the lies and temptations presented by Satan. By immersing ourselves in scripture and internalizing its truths, we equip ourselves with a formidable weapon against spiritual adversaries. The Word of God not only shields us from deception, but also empowers us to discern truth from falsehood and to walk in alignment with God's will.

In wielding the sword of the Spirit, we must cultivate a deep understanding of scripture and allow its truths to permeate every aspect of their lives. Through prayerful study and meditation on God's words, we sharpen the edge of our spiritual sword, enabling us to effectively combat the enemy's tactics. As we stand firm on the foundation of scripture, we find strength, courage, and victory in our spiritual battles, knowing that the Word of God is a steadfast defense and a mighty weapon against the forces of darkness.

The imperishable armor of God

God's armor is imperishable. It can withstand anything that comes in its way. This is an important fact. God never fails us. He always provides us with the strength we need to survive whatever comes our way. God's armor includes the power of faith. We have faith in God's protection and care. We also need to believe that He will guide and protect us in times of danger. Faith in God's protection is the best way to avoid trouble and stay safe. This means that no matter what happens, we will be okay. God protects and keeps us safe.

Ephesians 6:10-17 says, "Finally, be strong in the Lord and in his mighty power. Put on God's full armor so you can take your stand against the devil's schemes. For our struggle is not against flesh and blood, but against the rulers, against the authorities, against the cosmic powers over this present darkness and against the spiritual forces of evil in the heavenly realms. Therefore put on the full armor of God so that when the day of battle comes, you may be able to stand your ground and after you have done everything, to stand. Stand firm then, with the belt of truth buckled around your waist, with the breastplate of righteousness in place, and with your feet fitted with the readiness that comes from the gospel of peace. In addition to all this, take up the shield of faith, with which you can extinguish all the flaming arrows of the evil one. Take the helmet of salvation and the sword of the Spirit, which is the word of God."

Psalm 34:8-12 reminds us that, "I will say of the Lord, "He is my refuge and my fortress, my God, in whom I trust." Surely, he will save you from the fowler's snare and from the deadly pestilence. He will cover you with his feathers, and under his wings you will find refuge; his faithfulness will be your shield and rampart. You will not fear the terror of night, nor the arrow that flies by day, nor the pestilence that stalks in the darkness, nor the plague that destroys at midday. A thousand may fall at your side, ten thousand at your right hand, but it will not come near you. You will only observe with your eyes and see the punishment of the wicked. If you say, "The Lord is my refuge," and you make the Most High your dwelling, no harm will overtake you, no disaster will come near your tent. For he will command his angels concerning you to guard you in all your ways; they will lift you up in their hands, so that you will not strike your foot against a stone. You will tread on the lion and the cobra; you will trample the great lion and the serpent. "Because he loves me," says the Lord, "I will rescue him; I will protect him, for he acknowledges my name. He will call on me, and I will answer him; I will be with him in trouble, I will deliver him and honor him. With long life I will satisfy him and show him my salvation."

Isaiah 41:10-12 assures, "So do not fear, for I am with you; do not be dismayed, for I am your God. I will strengthen you and help you;

I will uphold you with my righteous right hand. "All who rage against you will surely be ashamed and disgraced; those who oppose you will be as nothing and perish. Though you search for your enemies, you will not find them. Those who wage war against you will be as nothing at all."

2 Corinthians 10:3-5 says, "For though we walk in the flesh, we are not waging war according to the flesh. For the weapons of our warfare are not carnal but mighty through God for pulling down strongholds, casting down arguments and every high thing that stands in their way."

The Bible assures that those who embrace the armor of God will never be defeated by the devil's plots. God's power enables the armor bearer to battle against the dark powers of this world.

Neglecting the Armor: Dire Consequences Ahead

As discussed above, we must not forget God's armor. This is important for remembering trials and temptations. If we do not wear the armor of God, we are most likely defeated by our enemies. The armor of God consists of spiritual weapons that help resist sin and temptation. These weapons empower us to have faith in Jesus Christ, experience repentance, and indulge in a prayerful life. When put on, these tools help overcome any obstacles that come into our way.

Job faced some difficult challenges, but he never forgot that he had the armor of God—His protection. Typically, we underestimate the importance of taking precautions in everyday life. Nevertheless, just as Job encounters daunting challenges, many individuals are currently grappling with difficult situations. If we remain vigilant, we recognize that God has equipped us with protective gear to shield us from the hardships and struggles of this sinful world.

We must be mindful of what protects us spiritually. We receive protection from God when we pray and place trust in Him. The Bible says, "Trust in the Lord with all your heart and lean not on your own understanding; In all your ways acknowledge Him, and He will make your paths straight" (Pro 3:5). When we rely on God and follow His guidance, He provides us with everything we need to face, and any challenging life brings our way.

Job faced immense challenges, but never wavered in his trust in God's protection. God has equipped us with armor to shield us from the hardships and difficulties of life. It is essential to recognize that we are not alone in our struggles, and that God is always by our side.

Furthermore, it is crucial to acknowledge that we have never been alone in our struggle. God's faithful followers have consistently been there for us, and we can count on Him to grant us the courage and fortitude necessary to confront adversity and to emerge victorious.

Overcoming Sins with the Armor of God

God equipped us with a powerful armor to shield us from evil. However, we cannot simply put on this armor and forget it; rather, it is a daily habit that requires constant maintenance. One effective way to guard ourselves against sin is to understand the impact of our sins. Our sins can inflict pain on relationships, spiritual journeys, and emotions. To counteract these adverse effects, we must understand the consequences of our sins.

It is not within our power to act independently, and we must depend on God to safeguard. We cannot venture forward without trust in Jesus Christ.

It is essential to be steadfast when adhering to God's directives. We must not only follow His commands because they are correct but also because they offer us protection.

The devil's cunning strategy is to lead us into sinning. By breaking God's law, we incur guilt and put ourselves at risk. God desires repentance and obedience to His commands, but He also extends forgiveness. This forgiveness is made possible through His Son, Jesus Christ. When we acknowledge our wrongdoing and seek forgiveness, God wipes away the guilt and shame that come with sinning. It is crucial to keep in mind that the devil thrives on feelings of shame and guilt.

Adhering to God's commandments can mitigate the repercussions of sin. Upholding a righteous lifestyle is crucial to fostering a positive relationship with Him. Engaging in simple practices such as prayer, Bible reading, and spending time with Him are vital ways to demonstrate obedience. When we heed God's guidance, He safeguards us from danger and helps us in overcoming any allurements that may arise. If you are grappling with sin, it is essential to seek solace in prayer and confide in a trusted Christian friend. By sharing your burden, you have already won half the battle. God can empower you to surmount your struggles and lead a life that aligns with His desires.

Therefore, it is crucial to limit the time and energy towards temptation. Setting realistic boundaries and being mindful of vulnerabilities are important. For instance, research has shown that loneliness often fuels temptations and the sin of pornography (Hesse & Floyd 2019). Therefore, surrounding ourselves with a supportive Christian community and engaging in social and spiritual activities can significantly reduce the likelihood of succumbing to temptation. Additionally, avoiding situations in which we are alone with our weaknesses is wise. Having an accountability partner or someone to lean on when faced with temptation can provide invaluable support for resisting allure.

Understanding the reasons behind our temptation can help us to resist it better. For example, if we are drawn to drugs or pornography because they provide temporary pleasure, we can seek alternative sources of fulfillment that do not involve sin. Once we understand the root cause of our temptation, it becomes easier to overcome it with the help of prayer for strength. We can ask God for courage and guidance to resist temptation, knowing that He is always there to support us.

I have struggled with various addictions in the past. One evening in 2007 stands out in my memory as I knelt to pray for the first time. I prayed to God, whom I knew little about, asking for deliverance from the temptation of addiction. To my surprise, one fine day, I realized that I had not smoked for two days. It was then that I realized that God had answered my prayer. However, it was up to me to resist and avoid contact with these addictions. I decided to cut ties with those who frequently dragged me back into my addiction. I have concluded that by recognizing our weaknesses and transforming them into strengths, we have the power to overcome any obstacles with God's help.

We must always seek assistance when attempting to overcome temptations. One source of support is seeking God's strength and direction. By confessing our sins to Him and seeking forgiveness, we can receive cleansing power that eliminates any guilt or shame associated with our transgressions. The devil feeds on our guilt and shame, using them to undermine our spiritual strength, which is our spiritual armor, and devours us with feelings of unworthiness. Furthermore, God offers a fresh start by promising to forgive us and transform our lives for better when we repent.

Seek divine assistance during times of temptation. If you find yourself struggling with temptation while praying, it is important to reach out to God to help in overcoming it. Lead a life of obedience to God's commandments, and He will surely forgive you and transform your life for better.

Follow the Divine Orders

When we understand our enemy well, their plans, and where they are weak, we should wrap ourselves in God's direction. These directions show us how to go about life. When we follow these rules, we grow closer to God and live happier lives. There are at least four special rules that can help you live happily and with purpose. The Psalmist assures that "God's words are like a light that shows me where to walk and what to do" (Ps 119:105). The book of Proverbs advice to "Trust God with all your heart. Don't try to figure things out on your own. Talk to Him in everything you do, and He will help you find the right path" (Pro 3:5-6). Jeremiah 29:11 says, "I have plans to give you a good future," says God. "I don't want to bring you harm, only hope." In the New Testament, Matthew says, "Put God first in everything you do, and He will give you all you need" (Matt 6:33). Adhering to God's divine commands enables us to withstand the assault of the devil. The following four divine orders strengthen faith.

The first divine order is ***love***. Love is the most powerful force in the universe that can transform pain into happiness and create beauty out of chaos. However, the practice of love is complex in nature. Humans tend to become overly critical. We quickly chose who we liked and disliked. Love is so magnificent that when we express it, we resemble God. On the contrary, "hating" or "not loving" someone is not a godly expression. This is an expression of a devil. He represents everything God is not. This enviousness instigated him to hate God, His creations and Jesus Christ. When we love someone, we connect them to the divine God, weakening the devil and evil plots of division and hate. This connection fulfills the greater purpose of God in our lives, as we unite and combat darkness with love and unity. The Bible says, "Let all that you do be done with love" (1 Cor 16:14). Through love's connective power, we embody the divine, thwarting the forces of hate and discord and fulfilling God's ultimate plan for unity and fellowship.

The second divine order to follow is ***peace***. Peace goes beyond feeling calm; it means being free from worry and fear. When you have peace, life flows smoothly, making you feel calm both inside and out. Peace brings contentment and harmony to your mind, body, and spirit, allowing God's energy to fill your life with joy and create meaningful experiences. Choosing peace is like taking a key step towards achieving your dreams and living the way God wants you to. In John 14:27, Jesus says, "Peace I leave with you; my peace I give you. I do not give to you as the world gives. Do not let your hearts be troubled and do not be afraid." These words highlight the special kind of peace that Jesus offers, a peace that goes beyond what we typically understand, bringing a sense of spiritual calm that helps us fight fear and worry, leading to a deep sense of well-being and spiritual completeness. By making peace a central part of your life, you access a source of divine love and calmness that not only enhances your personal journey, but also spreads warmth and kindness to others and the world. Pursuing peace is not just about inner peace, but also about shining a light in a chaotic world, showing a path towards unity and spiritual fulfillment based on the peaceful and graceful nature of God. When you allow yourself to be in peace, God will fill your life with liveliness; thus, you begin seeing the richest experiences. This is the second step we must take to achieve our true goals and fulfil our purpose on earth.

The third divine order is ***contentment***. The journey from anger to peace, dissatisfaction to fulfillment, and worry to trust should ultimately lead to contentment. Moving from a state of anxiety to trust is a crucial transition. It is about expecting challenges, but having faith that, with Christ's strength, you will have the means to face them. Trust blossoms when you face difficulties with the assurance of Christ by your side. Like Paul, you can declare, "I have learned in whatever situation I am to be content!" Embracing Christ's authority joyfully, affirming His sufficiency boldly, and appreciating the blessings He has bestowed upon you are key elements in attaining contentment. With the strength derived from Christ within me, I can surmount any obstacles that cross my path (Phil 4:13). Contentment is not merely a passive state of being satisfied with what you have, but an active choice to trust God's provision and guidance. It involves finding peace and joy in every circumstance, knowing that God's strength is available to help overcome any challenges that come your way. By acknowledging Christ's authority over your life, recognizing His sufficiency in all things, and cultivating a spirit of gratitude for His blessings, one can cultivate a deep sense of contentment that transcends external circumstances. This contentment rooted in faith allows you to face life's trials with resilience, knowing that you are not alone and that God's strength empowers you to endure and grow through adversity.

Fourth, but by no means last, the divine order is to practice ***forgiveness*** towards oneself and others. As humans, we are prone to making mistakes, hurting those dear to us, and veering off the course of righteous living. When we promptly cultivate the ability to forgive ourselves and those around us, we liberate precious time and energy to nurture love in our hearts and relationships. Ephesians 4:32 urges us, "And be kind to one another, tenderhearted, forgiving one another, even as God in Christ forgave you." Forgiveness is a powerful act that not only frees one forgiven, but also liberates the one who forgives. By releasing resentment, grudges, and past hurts, we open spaces in our hearts for healing, understanding, and compassion. Embracing forgiveness allows us to move forward with lighter hearts, fostering deeper connections with others. Just as God, through Christ, extends forgiveness to us despite our imperfections and shortcomings, we are called upon to reflect this divine grace in our interactions with one another. Forgiving oneself can be particularly challenging, as we often hold on to self-criticism and guilt. However, by offering ourselves the same grace and compassion that we extend to others, we can break free from the chains of self-doubt and self-condemnation, allowing for personal growth and spiritual renewal. Through the practice of forgiveness, we not only emulate the divine love and mercy that God shows us, but also create a space for healing, reconciliation, and transformation in our lives and relationships.

By mastering the knowledge and skills required to implement these four principles effectively, we can establish a harmonious rhythm in your life. This balance not only brings more prosperity but also speeds up the arrival of positive changes, leading to faster realization of one's desires and goals in alignment with God.

Gathering against the devil

The devil is undoubtedly a strong enemy that one must resist and fight every glance and breath. It should not misunderstand the devil with a battle aloud but rather a silent struggle. If armed with knowledge of God and perseverance in faith, one can permanently vanquish evil.

First, it is crucial to remember what we learned in Chapter One: the devil is an evil spirit who initially refuses to serve God and rebels against Him. Our efforts to battle the devil should focus on him, rather than on specific individuals or entities.

To battle the devil, we must first "gather around." The most powerful weapon is gathering and uniting against an invisible enemy. The enemy gains strength through dissonance. He used it to instill conflicts, misunderstandings, egos, and selfishness. Therefore, as we determine to battle the devil, we must gather in unity to support, serve, and survive. Remember, the heaven is for all. We are not going alone but with friends, family, and peers. God desires unity for us. "Finally, be ye all of one mind, having compassion one of another, love as brethren, be pitiful, be courteous" (1 Peter 3:8)

Next is prayer. Prayers can be used to ask for help against evil, forgiveness, and guidance. Again, praying united without ceasing is more powerful. Additionally, prayer can be a powerful tool for strengthening relationships between God and fellow believers. The early church experienced the outpouring of the Holy Spirit because they were united in prayers in one accord (Acts 2).

Another practice for fighting the devil is fasting. Fasting can help purge the body from impurities that may aid the devil in his work and provide spiritual nourishment and strength. Additionally, fasting can help connect more deeply with God during struggles. When Daniel needed God, he fasted up. "Then I set my face towards the Lord God to make a request by prayer and supplications, with fasting, sackcloth, and ashes" (Daniel 9:3). Fasting together is an incredibly potent method for combating the devil. When believers come together and engage in fasting and prayer, truly miraculous events can occur. The bible records of an amazing incidence in Acts 12:5-11,

> "So Peter was kept in prison, but the church was earnestly praying to God for him. The night before Herod was to bring him to trial, Peter was sleeping between two soldiers, bound with two chains, and sentries stood guard at the entrance. Suddenly an angel of the Lord appeared and a light shone in the cell. He struck Peter on the side and woke him up. "Quick, get up!" he said, and the chains fell off Peter's wrists. Then the angel said to him, "Put on your clothes and sandals." And Peter did so. "Wrap your cloak around you and follow me," the angel told him. Peter followed him out of the prison, but he had no idea that what the angel was doing was really happening; he thought he was seeing a vision. They passed the first and second guards and came to the iron gate leading to the city. It opened for them by itself, and they went through it. When they had walked the length of one street, suddenly the angel left him. Then Peter came to himself and said, "Now I know without a doubt that the Lord has sent his angel and rescued me from Herod's clutches and from everything the Jewish people were hoping would happen."

Therefore, it is crucial to keep in mind that the devil is not invincible. Despite his efforts to use temptations and fears to surrender, in unity with patience and perseverance, you can surmount them.

Uniting in Faith, United in Loyalty to God

Christians are called upon to unite our faith and loyalty to God, for in this unity lies our strength against the schemes of the devil. Scripture reminds us of Ecclesiastes 4:12 that, "though one may be overpowered, two can defend themselves. A cord of three strands is not quickly broken." Indeed, when we stand together in faith, we become fortified of enemy attacks.

Recognizing that the devil is a spiritual being, we can understand that our battle against him cannot be fought alone. In Ephesians 6:12, we are reminded that "our struggle is not against flesh and blood, but against the rulers, against the authorities, against the powers of this dark world and against the spiritual forces of evil in the heavenly realms." Thus, we must rely on the strength and assistance of our Heavenly Father to overcome the adversary.

By uniting faith and loyalty to God, we not only fortify ourselves against the devil's attacks, but also cultivate virtues of kindness, patience, and compassion towards one another. In Galatians 6:2, we are instructed to "carry each other's burdens, and in this way, you will fulfill the law of Christ." In this spirit of unity, we support and uplift one another, knowing we are fighting together on behalf of God.

Participating in church activities and studying the Word of God together further strengthens our bond with each other and with God. As it says in Proverbs 27:17, "As iron sharpens iron, so one person sharpens another." Through fellowship and mutual edification, we grow closer to God and become vital allies in battle against the devil.

Despite the challenges that we face, we are assured of victory through our unity in Christ. As it is written in Romans 8:37, "in all these things we are more than conquerors through him who loved us." The devil seeks to divide and sow discord among us, but we must stand firm in our unity, resisting his attempts to thwart God's purposes.

Together, we must pray fervently to seek God's guidance and protection in our battle against the enemy. Let us immerse ourselves in the Scriptures, equipping ourselves with the armor of God to withstand the devil's schemes (Ephesians 6:10-18). By unwavering faith and steadfast resolve, we will overcome every obstacle and emerge victoriously in Christ.

Fighting Against Satan

It is now time to brace ourselves to confront the devil. Let us consider a moment to reflect on the lessons learned. Unfortunately, we are still in the dark about the devil's intentions and we must always remain vigilant. First, it is essential to join forces to eliminate the common opposition. This enemy, who seeks to undermine our efforts, must be collectively confronted. We cannot hope to overcome him alone, so we must stand united and lend support to each other. Second, we must implement divine assistance in our struggles against the devil. By entreating God for strength and guidance, we can fortify our resolve and bolster our defenses. Prayers have long been regarded as potent weapon in the battle against the devil. Third, it is imperative that we possess an unwavering faith in God. Without this belief, we are unlikely to have prevailed against the devil. Therefore, we must have complete confidence in Him and trust that He will help us with our struggles. Fourth, we must thoroughly study the Bible to comprehend God's plans. This sacred text is replete with invaluable insights into how to defeat the devil. By immersing ourselves in its teachings, we can acquire the fortitude necessary to confront him. Fifth, we must confess our sins and renounce Satan. By acknowledging our transgressions and seeking God's forgiveness, we can overcome our vulnerabilities and more effectively resist the devil's allure. Finally, we must lead our lives in accordance with God's commandments. This approach will enable us to remain focused on and committed to the goal of vanquishing our adversary. The struggle against the devil is formidable, and we must stand together and ensure that he never emerges victorious!

Dominating Activities Against the Devil

Engaging in strategic and proactive measures against the devil requires a multifaceted approach akin to military operations. We must equip ourselves with spiritual weapons and strategies designed to thwart the devil's schemes and dismantle his strongholds.

Take control of the situation

If you find yourself feeling overwhelmed by the devil in your life, it is important to take proactive steps to regain control. First, remind yourself that the devil is not more powerful than God; he is simply an evil force in this world. The Bible assures us in James 4:7, "Submit yourselves, then to God. Resist the devil, and he will flee from you." By aligning ourselves with God's authority and resisting the devil's influence, we assert control over our lives.

Second, we must recognize that the devil seeks to exert control through fear, anxiety, and spiritual vulnerability. However, as believers, we are called upon to combat these negative emotions with faith and trust in God's promises. Philippians 4:6-7 encourages us, "Do not be anxious about anything, but in every situation, by prayer and petition, with thanksgiving, present your requests to God. And the peace of God, which transcends all understanding, will guard your hearts and your minds in Christ Jesus." By focusing on positive thoughts and relying on God's strength, we can overcome fear and anxiety.

Finally, cultivate resilience and strength, both mentally and physically, to withstand the devil's attacks. Ephesians 6:10-11 admonishes us, "Finally, be strong in the Lord and in his mighty power. Put on the full armor of God so that you can take your stand against the devil's schemes." By nurturing spiritual and physical well-being, we equip ourselves to resist the devil's attempts to control our lives.

Ultimately, remember that you are in control of your own spirituality. Do not allow the devil to sway over life. If you find yourself struggling with the influence of the devil, seek guidance from God. With faith, determination, and reliance on God's strength, one can break free from the chains of the devil's influence and walk in the freedom and victory that Christ has secured for one.

De-weaponize the Devil

To disarm the devil, Christians must engage the Word of God as their primary weapon through daily scripture reading, memorization, and the dissemination of its teachings. Prayers become a powerful shield that draws us closer to God, enables them to resist temptation, and banishes anxieties. A life characterized by compassion, forgiveness, and service to humanity is a formidable barrier to devils' evil plans. By obeying God's commands, helping others, and relying on divine power, we not only safeguard ourselves but also courageously confront the devil, secure in the knowledge of God's all-powerful protection.

The battle against the devil is fought on multiple fronts with faith, prayer, and good deeds, thus constituting a formidable arsenal. By immersing oneself in God's words, we can acquire an understanding and power. We may find comfort, resist temptation, and overcome doubts through fervent prayer. The light of a righteous existence dispels the darkness of the devil's plot.

Importantly, we do not fight this conflict alone. We have unwavering support from the Almighty God, which enables us to withstand attacks by the enemy. This divine relationship gives believers confidence to confront evil, knowing that they are shielded by God's affection and protection.

Christians must therefore continue their faithful voyages, arming themselves with God's words, bolstering their prayer, and living righteously. In this enduring conflict, our steadfast faith in God is a decisive factor that ensures that the devil's weapons are shattered eternally in the face of our staunch faith.

Conclusion

It is essential to understand that the devil is a predator and will try to use any opportunity to attack us to destroy our image in front of God. This means that it is crucial to be aware of our surroundings and to stay on the guard. Being positive and focused on what we want to achieve is important, as it will help us resist temptation and stay in control. Finally, it is important to have God's help dominate the devil. His power can help us overcome obstacles and his guidance can help us achieve our goals. It is essential to be aware of our surroundings and stay on guard, but by using positive reinforcement and God's power, we can overcome obstacles.

To dominate the activities against the devil, it is important to focus on three aspects: motivation, surroundings, and goals. We are more likely to succeed when motivated by good reasons such as helping others or achieving a goal. You should also surround yourself with supportive people who will help you achieve spiritual goals. Having God's help in dominating activities against the devil is crucial; his power and guidance can help achieve spiritual goals.

Remember that God is on your side. He will help you triumph over your enemy and provide you with the strength to do so. Pray for guidance and wisdom as you face your enemy. Ask the Lord to help you discover their weaknesses and attack those they are vulnerable to. Finally, be prepared to receive His victory! Above all, do not forget the armor of God.

Chapter 5

Exercising Faith

> *"I have fought the good fight, I have finished the race, I have kept the faith."*
> ***2 Timothy 4:7***

Faith emerges as a potent weapon amidst the stringent complexities of spiritual warfare. It goes beyond mere faith and serves as an effective safeguard against myriad attacks by the devil. As we navigate through the dense thicket of challenges thrown at by evilpowers, it is crucial to reinforce our belief in a higher power. Our faith in God's all-powerful and ever-present nature empowers us to persevere through the trials and tribulations that the dark forces try to impose upon us. This faith becomes the beacon of hope in pitch darkness, guides one's voyage into the lurking shadows, and protects one from damnation.

When faced with the enticing allure of deception and falsehoods crafted by the devil, faith empowers us to resist and remain steadfast, grounded in the unwavering and enduring love for God. The apostle Paul states in Ephesians 6:16, "above all, taking the shield of faith with which you will be able to quench all the fiery darts of the wicked one." Amidst a roaring tide of tribulations, faith reassures hope and futility against dark forces. Consistent nurturing maintains the vitality of faith and revitalizes independence in God's vows and blessings. Hebrews 11:6 affirms, "But without faith it is impossible to please Him, for he who comes must believe that He is, and that He is a reward of those who diligently seek Him". In a clash with the devil, our faith remains our best ally; it suffices above the dark lies and fallacies to proclaim conquest and deliverance in God's omniscience. Thus, let us fortify and place our full dependence on faith, a record of victory. In this chapter, we delve into the concept of faith and its practical application in our lives.

Exploring Faith

Faith serves as a steadfast anchor in the ever-changing landscape of life, providing stability and guidance amidst tempests of uncertainty. A study conducted by the PEW Research Center across 34 countries revealed that 45% of respondents believed in God, prayer, and moral values, which are all fundamental aspects of faith (Tamir et al., 2020). In times of difficulty, the essence of faith shines brightest, guiding individuals through the darkest valleys, and illuminating the path towards hope and renewal. "Now faith is confidence in what we hope for and assurance about what we do not see" (Heb 11:1).

The journey of faith is the odyssey of the soul, a pilgrimage of the divine that unfolds in moments of both triumph and tribulation. It is a journey that demands unwavering trust in the promises of God, even when storms of life rage around us. Paul reminds us that, "For we live by faith, not by sight" (2 Cor 5:7).

True faith is characterized by an active pursuit of God's truth and righteousness rather than passive acquiescence. It entails a dedication to following His will, even in the face of uncertainty or ambiguity. "And without faith it is impossible to please God because anyone who comes to him must believe that he exists and that he rewards those who earnestly seek him" (Heb 11:6).

In the crucible of life's trials and tribulations, faith emerges as the most potent weapon against forces of darkness. It empowers us to stand firm in the face of adversity, to press on with courage and determination, and embrace hope that lies beyond the horizon. "I have fought the good fight, I have finished the race, I have kept the faith" (2 Tim 4:7). We need to be encouraged to press on with unwavering confidence, knowing that our Heavenly Father is faithful enough to guide us along the path of righteousness.

Scriptures about faith

Faith is the cornerstone of the Christian journey, allowing believers to move through life's complexities to secure knowledge of God's plan (Wilt et al., 2016). It is more than a passive belief but a lifestyle that influences our response to life's challenges and victories. James 2:17 captures the essence of faith most succinctly, asserts that faith without corresponding actions is dead—a mere belief without power. Belief that lacks power does not reflect faith.

Numerous biblical passages more clearly explain actions in faith. Isaiah 40:31 say, "But those who trust in the Lord will become strong again—like eagles that grow new feathers. They will run and not get weak. They will walk and not get tired." Romans 10:9-10, "If you openly say, "Jesus is Lord" and believe in your heart that God raised him from death, you will be saved. Yes, we believe in Jesus deep in our hearts, and so we are made right with God. And we openly say that we believe in him, and so we are saved."

Faith enables us to confront challenges with fortitude and expectation, for we know that we serve a faithful God who is always with us (Ps 100:5). When the tempest swells about us and our hearts succumb to unbelief, faith becomes our fortress, enabling us to transcend the temporary and walk in a triumph. As a result, to live by faith is to acknowledge our limited understanding and comprehend that God's method is far beyond our grasp. To live by faith is to step out in belief and be confident in the conviction that God guides and supplies His children. Faith also entails developing a close friendship with God our Creator, a relationship based on prayer, engagement with scriptures, and communion with other believers, permitting His word to take root in our hearts and uproot our whole lives from the inside out. Moreover, faith drives us out into the world as "light to the world," demonstrating compassion, love, and mercy to those in distress.

The Old Testament illustrates faith through the lives of individuals who believed in the promises of God despite the challenges that they were going through. A good example is Abraham, often referred to as the father of faith. Genesis 12 describes how God called him out of his country to go to the land that He would show him. Despite not knowing where he was going, Abraham obeyed and began his faith journey. God further tested Abraham's faith when He promised him that he would have a son in old age. Despite his and Sarah's old age, Abraham believed that God would enable him to bear a child as God had promised (Heb 11:11-12). Thus, Isaac, the child of this promise, was born. The third example of the Old Testament is Moses. The man is known to have doubted his ability to deliver Israelites from Egypt when God called him Him. However, as he saw the power of God through the burning bush and later witnessed His signs and wonders in Egypt, Moses's faith grew. He trusted God to deliver His people, as demonstrated by the opening of the Red Sea (Ex 14).

Faith is also profound in the New Testament. Jesus many times exclaimed individuals and His disciples for their faith because He knew how important faith was in the acquisition of God's power and blessings. A good example is a woman with an issue of blood flow. She reached for the hem of Jesus' garment during His healing journey, believing that she would be healed when she touched Him (Matt 9:20-22). Another example in the New Testament, which portrayed faith, was the Roman Centurion that impressed Jesus. The Roman centurion said, "Lord, I do not deserve to have you come under my roof. But just say the word, and my servant will be healed." Jesus said, "Truly I tell you, I have not found anyone in Israel with such great faith" (Matt 8:8-10). The way the centurion demonstrated humility and faith in Jesus' healing power, despite being far away, was a testament to his faith in Jesus' authority.

The New Testament Apostles demonstrated faith through steadfast preaching on Jesus. Initially, the apostle Peter had a shaky faith, notably when he denied Jesus three times before crucifixion. However, after the resurrection of Jesus Christ, Peter's faith transformed. He began to preach without fear, becoming a strong and courageous proclaimer of the gospel and performing several miracles, as recorded in Acts 1:12-28.

The aspects of faith in both the New and Old Testaments are vital realities in Christians' lives. Faith is not merely about holding certain beliefs, but entails a profound, implicit trust in God's words. This trust empowers believers to act boldly, as demonstrated by Peter and others in the New Testament.

Moreover, faith propels us to pray and offer intercession on the premise that God is sovereign and can work every little for good. Jesus, on his piece to His disciplines, told them in Matthew 21:22 that "When you pray, you can get anything you need if you have faith". When we pray for and ponder God's promise in His message, our faith is strengthened, giving us the ability to move boldly and with certainty into his provision. Faith is an intrinsic guide to the existence of a Christian journey through the unknown in this world.

Faith plays a vital role in the entirety of the Bible, demonstrating the love of God and the importance of those who place trust and faith in Him. Scriptures repeatedly affirm that a person can overcome diverse obstacles and trials, fight personal wars, and win spiritual battles against the devil due to faith. Furthermore, faith is the power that changes our mindset and assists us in living differently, since, according to Hebrews 11:1, it is the guarantee of what we long for, the conviction of what we do not see. "Now faith is the substance of things hoped for, the evidence of things not seen." When we unconditionally trust the Lord, we literally call Him and his attention and involvement, due to which we weather the storms of life with more courage and persistence. As is well known, faith shields as confirmed in Ephesians 6:16 individuals "with which you can distinguish all the flammable arrows of the evil one."

Neutralizing Demonic Activities through Faith

In spiritual battlefields, faith emerges as one of the most powerful weapons against demonic influences. The Bible teaches us that faith is not just belief;

it is a powerful agent, which, if used right, can walk you through second to none and show you the righteous way. 1 Peter 1:5 says, "who through faith are shielded by God's power until the coming of the salvation that is ready to be revealed in the last time."

Power of Faith

Faith is powerful; it can transform life and help you through some of the toughest times. When you have faith in God, yourself, and in what you believe in, you can take on any challenge that comes your way. Here is what faith can do for us.

1. ***Faith gives you hope***: When things seem harsh, having faith in yourself and your goals can help you keep going. Even when things look impossible, remember that there is always a chance of success if you keep pushing forward. Isaiah 40:31 says, "but those who hope in the Lord will renew their strength. They will soar on wings like eagles; they will run and not grow weary, they will walk and not be faint."
2. ***Faith can help you focus on your goals***: When you have faith in yourself and your abilities, you are more likely to stay focused on your goals, which will help you achieve them faster and with less effort. As Philippians 4:13 reminds us, "I can do all things through Christ who strengthens me."
3. ***Faith can give you strength when things get tough***: Having faith in yourself and your goals can help you stay strong when things go wrong. Recall that everything will work out if you keep moving forward. Psalm 27:1 encourages us, "The Lord is my light and my salvation; whom shall I fear? The Lord is the stronghold of my life; of whom shall I be afraid?"
4. ***Faith can help you to be patient***: When things take longer than expected or when there are obstacles in your way, having faith in yourself and your goals can help you to be patient. Recall that it takes time to achieve something great, but eventually, it will happen. James 1:3-4 tells us, "For you know that the testing of

your faith produces steadfastness. And let steadfastness have its full effect, that you may be perfect and complete, lacking in nothing."

5. ***Faith can help you be optimistic about the future***: When things look bleak, having faith in yourself and your goals can help you see the future as a positive place. Remember that anything is possible if you continue to work hard. Jeremiah 29:11 assures us, "For I know the plans I have for you, declares the Lord, plans for welfare and not for evil, to give you a future and a hope."
6. ***Faith helps you stay positive***: Even when things are tough, having a positive attitude can help you see the good in everything. This will help you stay focused and motivated, even when everything else seems wrong. Romans 12:12 advises us, "Rejoice in hope, be patient in tribulation, be constant in prayer."
7. ***Faith encourages perseverance***: When things get tough, we sometimes give up on our goals. Faith allows us to persevere, even when things seem impossible. This makes it easier to achieve our goals. Hebrews 12:1 encourages us, "Therefore, since we are surrounded by so great a cloud of witnesses, let us also lay aside every weight, and sin which clings so closely, and let us run with endurance the race that is set before us."
8. ***Faith gives you strength***: When things become tough, having faith in yourself and your goals can give you the power to fight back. This strength will help overcome any obstacles that come in your way. Psalm 18:2 declares, "The Lord is my rock and my fortress and my deliverer, my God, my rock, in whom I take refuge, my shield, and the horn of my salvation, my stronghold."
9. ***Faith can help you be grateful***: When things are tough, it can be easy to forget all the good things in life. Having faith in yourself and your goals can help you be grateful for everything happening, which will help you maintain a positive attitude and remain motivated. 1 Thessalonians 5:18 instructs us, "Give thanks in all circumstances; for this is the will of God in Christ Jesus for you."
10. **Faith can help you find peace**: When things are tough, it can help you find peace. This peace can help you stay calm and focus

on difficult times. Philippians 4:7 promises, "And the peace of God, which surpasses all understanding, will guard your hearts and your minds in Christ Jesus."

Waiting upon God

Waiting upon God is essential to faith, and it means trusting Him to do what He promised He will do. Waiting upon God can be difficult at times, but it is always worth it in the end. Waiting upon God means living in hope, and we can find hope in many different places in the Bible.

Psalm 34:18-19 says, "The Lord is my strength and my song; he has become my salvation; he is my fortress, and my Deliverer; my God, who helps me, and my Redeemer." Apostle Paul also wrote about waiting on God in Philippians 4:6-7: "Do not be anxious about anything, but in everything by prayer and supplication with thanksgiving let your requests be made known to God. And the peace of God, which transcends all understanding, will guard your hearts and minds in Christ Jesus."

Some of the most famous scriptures about putting your faith in God are from Psalm 34:18-19: "The Lord is my strength and my song; he has become my salvation; he is my fortress, and my Deliverer; my God, who helps me, and my Redeemer." Apostle Paul also wrote about putting your faith in God in Philippians 4:6-7: "Do not be anxious about anything, but in everything by prayer and supplication with thanksgiving let your requests be made known to God. And the peace of God, which transcends all understanding, will guard your hearts and your minds in Christ Jesus."

Putting faith in God is the foundation of trust. Scripture tells us that without faith, it is impossible to please God (Heb 11:6). We can put our faith in God by obeying Him and doing what He says. Scripture also tells us that faith comes from hearing and hearing through the Word of God (Rom 10:17). We can find comfort and guidance in the scriptures, and by putting our faith in God, we can be sure that He will help us through whatever comes our way.

Exercising Faith against Evil

With our faith in God, we have successfully neutralized demonic activities. Moving forward, faith can be utilized as a powerful tool to guard ourselves against evil forces. Faith is a fundamental aspect of Christian Walk and indispensable when confronting evil. Facing spiritual challenges, we must remember that God is ever present and can be relied upon to overcome our difficulties. By adopting this perspective, we can exhibit our trust in God and fortify our determination to resist evil.

We must rely on our faith to help us overcome evil. Remember that the Heavenly Father is with you and will always be. He will help you overcome obstacles and achieve goals. Use whatever method works best to build faith against evil. Keep a positive attitude and focus on what you can do to help others. When faced with difficult situations, focusing on negative situations is easy. Instead, we should remember that positive things are always happening in the world. We can think about suffering people and try to do something to help them. We can also focus on the blessings in our lives and remind ourselves that everything will ultimately work out. Doing these can increase our chances of success and maintain a positive attitude during difficult times.

Exercising faith in God

Ability to Resist Evil

Faith is a vital element in an individual's life. It often serves as a source of solace and support while trying circumstances, providing the necessary encouragement to persevere during challenging times. When people have faith, they understand that there is something greater than themselves, and they can rely on this higher power to help them through difficult times. However, despite having faith, some people may still struggle with evil. Thus, the ability to resist evil is crucial. Having faith does not imply that a person is immune to the effects of sin. A person can have faith in God or another higher power but is still susceptible to the influence of evil.

A person's ability to resist evil is based on strength and morality. Some people may be able to resist the effects of evil more than others, and this ability varies from person to person. Some may find it easier to fight evil because they have firm beliefs in God. Others may effectively resist evil because they adhere to a strong moral code. It is essential for each person to understand their strengths and weaknesses in resisting evil and to use them to their advantage.

If you can resist evil, you will be moving in the right direction. Resisting evil requires not allowing oneself to be swayed by negative experiences in life. This means not giving in to feelings of resentment or wrath that you may experience. Additionally, it implies not allowing oneself to be driven by fear. If you can resist evil, you are taking a strong stand against what is harmful to the world. However, it is difficult to resist the effects of sins. It takes a lot of strength and willpower, and it can be challenging to stay strong when things are difficult. However, if you can resist evil, you are taking significant steps in the right direction.

It is important to remember that resisting evil is not easy. It takes a lot of strength and courage to remain strong in the face of danger. However, if you can do it, you will be able to protect yourself and those around you from harm. If you are facing a difficult situation in which you feel like you may be susceptible to the effects of evil, it is crucial to talk to someone about it. There are people who can help resist the effects of sin, and they can guide you in the right direction. If you struggle with the impact of evil, do not give up. Remember that having strong faith in God or another higher power does not mean that you are immune to the effects of evil. This means that you have strength and resilience. With sufficient determination and effort, the obstacles can be overcome.

Consider Joseph's story in the Old Testament as an example of resisting evil through faith and moral integrity. Joseph, the beloved son of Jacob, was sold into slavery by his jealous brothers. Despite this severe betrayal and hardship, Joseph maintained faith in God. He did not allow himself to overcome bitterness or hatred. Instead, he continued to trust God's plan for life.

While serving the house of Potiphar, Joseph faced another significant test. Potiphar's wife attempted to seduce him, but Joseph resisted her advances, saying, "How then can I do this great wickedness, and sin against God?" (Genesis 39:9). Joseph's faith and adherence to his moral principles gave him the strength to resist temptation, even when it led to false accusations and imprisonment.

Joseph continued to trust God in prison. His unwavering faith and integrity eventually led to his rise to power in Egypt, where he became second in command of the Pharaoh. When a famine struck the land, Joseph's leadership and wisdom, bestowed by God, saved many lives, including those of his family. When his brothers came to Egypt seeking food, Joseph forgave them, demonstrating his continued resistance to evil through choosing mercy over vengeance.

Joseph's story illustrates the power of faith in resisting evil. Despite numerous trials and temptations, Joseph's faith in God provided him with the strength and resilience required to overcome these challenges. His life serves as a testament to the fact that maintaining faith and moral integrity, even in the face of great adversity, can lead to the ultimate triumph and fulfilment of God's purposes.

Trust in God

Faith is more than just a belief in God. It is a conviction that the divine is absolute and will guide our lives. Faith can be expressed in various forms such as prayer, meditation, or any other form of contemplation. It can also be demonstrated through actions, such as helping others or simply living life to its fullest potential. There is no singular way to express faith as it varies from person to person. However, expressing faith in some form is a valuable way to connect with our spiritual side and seek guidance from the above. Ultimately, faith is about believing in ourselves and our path, rather than blindly following someone else's opinions.

Faith has numerous benefits. For instance, faith can help people live happier and healthier lives. Our beliefs can give us hope during times of difficulty, which aids in perseverance. Faith also helps us to connect with our spiritual selves and strengthens our self-confidence. Faith is a personal journey unique to everyone. However, expressing faith in some form is an essential step towards achieving happiness and fulfillment. No matter what we believe, we can gain strength and joy from faith. We must trust God and allow Him to lead our lives.

A profound example of faith in the Bible is Abraham's story. God promised Abraham that he would be the father of many nations, despite Abraham and his wife Sarah being advanced in age and childless (Gen 17:5). Abraham trusted in God's promise and continued to have faith even when the fulfillment of that promise seemed impossible. Sarah's faith was rewarded when Sarah miraculously gave birth to Isaac. This story demonstrates how unwavering faith in God's promises can lead to extraordinary outcomes even when circumstances appear insurmountable.

Submission to God's Providences

We often think of faith as something we cling to when things become tough, a source of strength to keep us going when everything seems to be falling apart. However, what if faith is more like muscle? What if we exercised our faith every day so that it grew stronger? This is the approach we should adopt in our faith in God. We should constantly seek ways to exercise and strengthen our faith, with the aim of continuous growth. This means being willing to endure tough times and trusting that God always has our best interests.

God has shown us time and time again that He is always working for the best. As Romans 8:28 reminds us, "And we know that in all things God works for the good of those who love him, who have been called according to his purpose." Therefore, let us trust Him and persistently exercise faith in Him.

Throughout our lives, there are countless moments when we can use faith to pull us through. We might face difficult circumstances, but we can find comfort in knowing that God is with us. Even when things do not go as we want, we can trust that God is orchestrating everything for our ultimate good. As Proverbs 3:5-6 advises, "Trust in the Lord with all your heart and lean not on your own understanding; in all your ways submit to him, and he will make your paths straight."

When times are difficult, it is easy to lose hope. However, by continually relying on God, we can find hope, even in the darkest moments. As our faith grows stronger, we see that everything starts to fall into place, no matter what happens. So, let us keep exercising our faith and trust that God always has our best interests at the heart. With sufficient effort and persistence, we can reach a point where our faith is so strong that nothing can bring us down.

Enabling Divine Authority

There is a prevailing trend in society where individuals increasingly embrace divine authority, which refers to the belief that individuals, paths, or beliefs can guide and direct their lives. Although the source of this power is unimportant to some, it is more focused on its benefits. People are frequently drawn to evil sources because they appear to be thriving, which is often because of their lack of knowledge. The outcomes of allying with a devil are not always beneficial. As shown throughout the book, the devil despises humanity because we were created by the holy God in His own image (Gen 1:27). Although it may seem like an alluring and expedient path to success, the devil's aim is not to promote well-being. 1 Peter 5:8 says, "Be sober-minded; be watchful. Your adversary the devil prowls around like a roaring lion, seeking someone to devour." God has ensured that we are protected from the devil's influence by creating an eternal enmity between us and the devil that prevents them from becoming friends. "And I will put enmity between you and the woman, and between your offspring and hers; he will crush your head, and you will strike his heel" (Gen 3:15). It is essential to keep in mind that, as children of God, we must demonstrate devotion and commitment to Him. No matter what stage of life you are in, there are advantages in acknowledging God's sovereignty.

1. ***Increased Confidence and Self-Belief***: Trusting in the knowledge and guidance of divine authority can enhance self-belief in both personal and spiritual matters. This confidence can provide the strength to face complex challenges and move forward, even when situations seem insurmountable. It can also help you see yourself as capable of achieving great things regardless of others' opinions.

*2. **Greater Sense of Purpose and Direction***: Finding your way in life can be a challenge if you lack clarity regarding what you are seeking. However, by relying on divine guidance from God, one can gain a deeper understanding of one's purpose in this world and how to achieve it. In this endeavor, seekers can discover their life's purpose, which can ultimately transform their spiritual life and lead to a more meaningful existence. This new understanding can provide a greater sense of direction in your life, enabling you to make more informed decisions about your actions and choices.

*3. **Improved Spiritual Growth***: Accepting divine authority as part of your spiritual growth process can help deepen your faith in God and develop a stronger connection with Him. This connection can provide strength and guidance during challenging times and help tap into more significant sources of inspiration and motivation. It can also help you connect with others who share your faith, provide support and inspiration during your spiritual journey—a church, a small prayer group, etc.

Understanding Divine Authority

Belief in God or gods has been a fundamental part of human history, dating back to ancient times when people sought explanations for the natural world. As humanity observed the patterns and connections in nature that eluded understanding, these beliefs evolved into what we now call faith. Although once labeled as superstitions, these early beliefs were deeply rooted in the human desire to understand and connect with a higher power. Today, seeking and desiring to believe in the divine spans across all cultures and religions.

To possess divine authority suggests that one holds the power believed to originate from God. This power is frequently perceived as an inherent attribute of the divine. Jesus, being the son of the Most High, wielded the divine authority of God during his ministry on earth. As both fully human and divine, Jesus exemplified the potency of divine authority to such an extent that he also granted us authority to employ it against the devil. "I have given you authority to trample on snakes and scorpions and to overcome all the power of the enemy; nothing will harm you" (Lk 10:19).

Despite the different interpretations of divine authority, some benefits can be gained by accepting it as part of spiritual growth. These benefits include increased spiritual confidence, greater sense of purpose, optimism, and improved spiritual growth. When you accept divine authority, you acknowledge that God's power exists, and that He can help guide and direct your life.

When you embrace divine authority, you may discover that it is simpler to tap into God's power. This is because by acknowledging the existence of divine authority, you are also accepting the responsibility that accompanies it. This responsibility involves being open to listening to and adhering to the guidance of this power, even if it may not seem to make sense initially. When you are eager to believe in the guidance of the divine authority, it can lead to new opportunities for personal development and advancement in your life. This development is transformative, guiding us towards prosperity in this life and readying us for future challenges.

So, what do you think? Do you believe that accepting divine authority can help boost spiritual growth? If so, why do you think embracing this belief system is important? In the next section, we examine its significance.

Miracles in the Bible: Witnessing Divine Authority

Miracles, manifestations of divine authority, are supernatural and often inexplicable events that provide evidence of divine intervention. These events can be experienced by individuals, groups, or entire nations, demonstrating the power and presence of higher authority. Despite the lack of scientific validation, beliefs in miracles are widespread and often inspire believers' devotion and awe. Miracles defy the laws of nature, such as a severely ill person healing without medical intervention or even dead people coming to life. Although this statement may sound superficial, it is faith that God's people have experienced miracles.

Before we delve into the miracles in the Bible, I feel compelled by the spirit to share a personal testimony of His miraculous intervention in my life. In 2014, I was diagnosed with leukaemia. Alone in Pune, Maharashtra, I found myself facing this daunting challenge with the support of only a professor and one friend. They accompanied me to the Ruby Cancer Center, where each day brought a new wave of fear and uncertainty. Never had I confronted the reality of death so closely.

One day, the doctor delivered a sobering message: I needed to bring my relatives and begin treatment immediately. The gravity of the situation was overwhelming and I felt as if my world was collapsing. That night, in my deepest despair, I knelt and prayed with an intensity and connection that I had never experienced before. This prayer exhibited divine authority and was an expression of faith, in opposition to the adversities of my life and in defiance of the devil who sought to consume me. In that moment of profound prayer, I felt an extraordinary closeness to God. I made a decision in that prayer—I would forgo further treatment and live by faith for as long as possible. Now, a decade has passed, and I am still here, alive, and filled with gratitude, praising God for this miraculous extension of life. God is good.

The Bible is filled with miracle accounts that exemplify the use of divine authority by various God's people, prophets, and saints. Miracles performed by God, as recorded in the Bible, highlight the application of divine authority to heal the sick, move objects, and raise the dead. The resurrection of Jesus Christ (Jn 11:25-26) and His transfiguration (Matt 17:1-3) are among the most renowned miracles, showcasing the ultimate power of divine authority over life and death. Other notable miracles include the healing of blindness (Jn 9:6-7), curing of leprosy (Lk 17:12-14), and exorcism of demons (Mk 5:1-13), all of which demonstrate the direct intervention of divine authority in human affairs.

These miracles serve as tangible evidence for God's omnipotence and His active involvement in the world. Many Christians believe that miracles continue to occur today, providing ongoing proof of God's presence, His intervention, and the enduring power of divine authority.

The Bible documents numerous instances in which divine authority is exercised through miracle. These accounts not only affirm the existence of a higher power, but also emphasize the role of divine authority in guiding and inspiring believers. Using divine authority, miraculous events in the Bible reinforce the faith of believers and underscore the profound impact of divine intervention in the natural world.

In the context of spiritual warfare, the divine authority is crucial. Ephesians 6:12 reminds us, "For our struggle is not against flesh and blood, but against the rulers, against the authorities, against the powers of this dark world and against the spiritual forces of evil in the heavenly realms." Believers are empowered to combat the spiritual forces of evil through divine authority. The miracles performed by Jesus, such as casting out demons (Mark 1:34), highlight the power of the divine authority in overcoming spiritual adversaries. By embracing and wielding divine authority, believers can stand firm in their faith and emerge victoriously in spiritual battle.

Thus, the use of divine authority is not only central to the occurrence of miracles, but also pivotal in the realm of spiritual warfare, providing believers with the strength and confidence to confront and overcome the forces of darkness.

Spiritual Gifts and Divine Authority

Divine authority is central to understanding and experiencing spiritual gifts. Everyone has a unique relationship with the divine, shaped by their heart, desires, and intentions. Spiritual gifts bestowed through divine authority help deepen the sacred connection. Some key spiritual gifts include the following.

1. **Prophecy**: Empowered by the divine authority, prophecy grants individuals the ability to foresee future events and offer warnings about potential dangers, providing guidance and protection. "In the last days, God says, I will pour out my Spirit on all people. Your sons and daughters will prophesy, your young men will see visions, your old men will dream dreams" (Acts 2:17). 2 Peter 1:21 says, "For prophecy never had its origin in the human will, but prophets, though human, spoke from God as they were carried along by the Holy Spirit."
2. **Healing**: This gift, granted through divine power, enables individuals to restore health and balance with others, whether they are individuals, groups, or entire communities, reflecting the healing nature of the divine.
3. **Guidance**: Rooted in divine wisdom, this gift allows people to help others make informed decisions and navigate their life paths, offering clarity and direction inspired by the divine.
4. **Inspiration**: Through divine influence, individuals with this gift can instill hope and encouragement in others, motivating them to pursue goals and overcome challenges.

Prayers are profound spiritual gifts that facilitate a deeper connection with the divine. It allows individuals to seek guidance, support, forgiveness, and peace, thus enriching their spiritual journey. Meditation is another valuable gift that aids in focusing on thoughts and connecting one's inner self. It offers insight into personal beliefs and values as well as an appreciation for the diversity of other cultures, all under the realm of divine reflection. Fasting serves as a powerful tool for spiritual growth, allowing individuals to connect more deeply to their spiritual hunger and divine essence. It embodies self-discipline and deeper yearning for the divine.

To discover and exercise your spiritual gift for wielding divine authority against evil entities, refer to the assessment tool in the Appendix (B) to identify your spiritual gift. The most effective way to uncover and strengthen this gift is to connect deeply with God through prayer, meditation, and fasting. These spiritual practices help attune your mind and soul to divine guidance, fostering a closer relationship with God, and empowering you to stand firm against evil. By committing to regular prayer, meditation, and fasting, you open yourself to receiving divine wisdom and strength, thus enabling you to harness your spiritual gift with greater authority and purpose.

Authority in the Bible

When it comes to divine authority, the Bible is clear: one God is sovereign and appoints certain people to represent Him on earth referred to as "prophets" and "apostles." The Bible teaches that God gives these people authority, allowing them to speak on His behalf and teach His Word.

For example, the apostles were tasked with preaching the gospel to all nations and overseeing the Christian church, which was ultimately responsible for leading people to Christ. As Ephesians 4:11-13 states, "So Christ himself gave the apostles, the prophets, the evangelists, the pastors and teachers, to equip his people for works of service, so that the body of Christ may be built up until we all reach unity in the faith and in the knowledge of the Son of God and become mature, attaining to the whole measure of the fullness of Christ."

Jesus, as a human, received the power and authority of God on earth, demonstrating the potential for any human to receive such power. Jesus was unique in that He was sinless and unblemished, possessing the ability to perform extraordinary feats such as raising the dead, restoring sight to the blind, making the lame walk, and forgiving sins on the cross, thereby reconciling humanity with God (Mk 2:5-12).

The Bible also teaches that God plans for His people, both individually and as a community. He has chosen specific people to shepherd His sheep, leading the church in righteousness and teaching them God's words while protecting them from harm. Paul emphasizes the qualities of such leaders in 1 Timothy 3:1-7, stating, "Here is a trustworthy saying: Whoever aspires to be an overseer desires a noble task. Now the overseer is to be above reproach, faithful to his wife, temperate, self-controlled, respectable, hospitable, able to teach, not given to drunkenness, not violent but gentle, not quarrelsome, not a lover of money."

The Bible emphasizes that believers can represent God by speaking on His behalf, imparting His Word, and directing people towards Christ. This representation and guidance was provided under the divine supervision of God. 2 Peter 1:20-21 explains, "Above all, you must understand that no prophecy of Scripture came about by the prophet's own interpretation of things. For prophecy never had its origin in the human will, but prophets, though human, spoke from God as they were carried along by the Holy Spirit."

As noted in 2 Timothy 1:9-10, "He has saved us and called us to a holy life—not because of anything we have done but because of his own purpose and grace. This grace was given us in Christ Jesus before the beginning of time, but it has now been revealed through the appearing of our Savior, Christ Jesus, who has destroyed death and has brought life and immortality to light through the gospel."

The Holy Spirit

The Holy Spirit is a cornerstone of Christian beliefs, playing an indispensable role in understanding and following Jesus Christ. According to Christian doctrine, the Holy Spirit is part of the Trinity, alongside the Father and the Son, and is crucial for living a Christ-centered life. Without the Holy Spirit, it would be impossible to fully grasp or adhere to Christ's teachings. The Holy Spirit is a gift from God, aiding believers in living according to God's will, and providing spiritual empowerment.

The Holy Spirit fills believers with spiritual power, enabling them to communicate with God, deepen their understanding of Him and obey His commands. Acts 2:38-39 emphasizes the Holy Spirit's role in the Christian journey: "Peter replied, 'Repent and be baptized, every one of you, in the name of Jesus Christ for the forgiveness of your sins. And you will receive the gift of the Holy Spirit.'" This passage highlights the Holy Spirit as a gift received upon repentance and baptism, which is crucial for a believer's spiritual life.

In Christian tradition, the Holy Spirit also equips believers for the ministry, teaching them about God and guiding them to live righteously. The Holy Spirit fosters spiritual growth and strengthens the relationship between believers and God. John 14:15-17 reflects this guiding role: "If you love me, keep my commands. And I will ask the Father, and he will give you another advocate to help you and be with you forever—the Spirit of truth."

Furthermore, the Holy Spirit's presence is marked by transformative power, enabling believers to speak in tongues and perform miracles, as seen in Acts 5:3-4: "And they were all filled with the Holy Spirit and began to speak in other tongues as the Spirit enabled them." However, the true evidence of the Holy Spirit's presence is seen in the transformation of character and the fruits of the Spirit as outlined in Galatians 5:22-23.

The Holy Spirit's guidance is essential to living a life that pleases God. Romans 8:9-13 elaborates on this, stating, "You, however, are not in the realm of the flesh but are in the realm of the Spirit, if indeed the Spirit of God lives in you. And if anyone does not have the Spirit of Christ, they do not belong to Christ." The following passage emphasizes the profound influence of the Holy Spirit, signifying a clear departure from being governed by one's sinful nature.

The Holy Spirit also plays a vital role in the interpretation of scriptures and prophecies. The Spirit inspired the prophets and apostles, guiding them to write the Bible and continues to guide believers in understanding its truths today. Many Christians believe that the writings of key historical figures in the church were guided by the Holy Spirit, thus providing valuable spiritual insights. These gifts through the Holy Spirit empower believers with the authority of God against the devil.

Repentance

Many people today find it difficult to trust God. They were taught to question and doubt everything that they believed. But, is this the best way to approach spirituality? Repentance is a change in the heart that leads someone to forsake sinful actions and desires. It is an act of contrition or sorrow for wronging God and His laws.

Repentance is a necessary step in returning to God and cleansing sin. The Bible teaches that repentance is essential for salvation. Although salvation is not contingent upon repentance, it is through repentance that one can initially purify and approach the divine presence of God, which is embodied in Jesus Christ, by placing faith in Him. Jesus, Himself said, "Unless you repent, you will all likewise perish" (Luke 13:3). Repentance is also mentioned many times in the Old and New Testaments. For example, in the book of Isaiah, we read, "The Lord says: 'If you return to me and obey my commandments and seek me with all your heart, I will give you rain from the heavens and the earth will yield its fruit'" (Isaiah 55:8-9). The command to "return" to God and "obey" Him is an act that is possible through repentance.

Repentance can help us trust and obey God. When we repented our sins and turned away from them, we demonstrated to God that we are sorry for what we have done wrong. This shows that we are willing to change and grow our relationship with God. God may allow us to experience His forgiveness and mercy, as we repent. He may also open up new opportunities in our lives. Repentance should not be viewed as a punishment or a required step to receive forgiveness. Instead, it is an act of humility and contrition that shows us that we are willing to change and grow our relationship with God.

It is often difficult for individuals to feel remorse or repentance when sin, which is a common human behavior. However, these feelings can arise naturally when someone is genuinely dedicated to seeking God's forgiveness and mending their relationship with Him. Repentance can be powerful in transforming lives and improving relationships with God and others. We need to repent our sins, as this will allow us to live more wisely and ethically, and to follow God more devotedly.

The concept of repentance is of utmost importance in mending our relationship with God. This enables us to have faith and to follow His guidance. By demonstrating a commitment to repentance, we can surmount obstacles that may present themselves in our lives, including sin, demonization, and demonic activities, as well as broader spiritual warfare. We will be able to live more wisely and ethically, and build healthy relationships with others. When we repent, we acknowledge our wrongdoing against God and others, promising to refrain from repeating these actions. This construction allows us to comprehend the wrongdoings and glean lessons from them. Furthermore, it can prompt us to yearn for God's forgiveness and expunge ourselves from every transgression. If you are struggling to believe in God, try repentance first. It can help open your heart to Him, allow Him to lead you on your path in life, and stabilize you in your spiritual journey.

Faith in Christ

When we come to faith in Christ, we trust not in our abilities, but in the abilities of the one who died for us—Jesus Christ. In this way, we enter a relationship with God that surpasses all other possibilities. This relationship allows us to be empowered by God and do great things for Him. To establish this relationship, we must be willing to let go of our ways and live for Christ. We must also be willing to forgive others and accept them into the community. Christ wants us to have a life full of love, joy, peace and happiness. Faith in Christ is a relationship with God that supersedes anything else we can ever hope for.

To have faith in Christ, we must be willing to let go of our way and live for Christ. We must also be willing to forgive others and accept them into the community. When we have faith in Christ, we can be sure that we are able to do great things for God. Christ wants us to have a life full of love, joy, peace and happiness. When we have faith in Christ, we can be sure that we will be able to do great things for our neighbors.

Through Prayers

Divine authority is one of the many gifts Jesus Christ bestowed on His Church. Through prayer, believers can cultivate a personal relationship with God, receive the power to accomplish His will, and harness the divine authority granted to them. Prayer is a powerful tool that builds faith, strengthens bonds with God, and intercedes on behalf of others.

In Matthew 21:22, Jesus emphasizes the power of prayer: "If you believe, you will receive whatever you ask for in prayer." This verse underscores the importance of faith in prayer, demonstrating that through prayer, believers can access divine authority and see God's will manifest in their lives.

Prayers can take many forms, and it is essential for each individual to find an approach that best facilitates their connection with God. Some may find solace in silent meditation, whereas others may prefer vocal prayer, communal prayer, or even prayer journaling. The key is to remain open and receptive to the guidance of the Heavenly Father. Philippians 4:6-7 advises, "Do not be anxious about anything, but in every situation, by prayer and petition, with thanksgiving, present your requests to God. And the peace of God, which transcends all understanding, will guard your hearts and your minds in Christ Jesus." This passage highlights the role of prayer in alleviating anxiety and bringing peace through divine intervention.

Prayer not only enhances our relationship with God, but also empowers us to lift others in prayer. James 5:16 states, "Therefore confess your sins to each other and pray for each other so that you may be healed. The prayer of a righteous person is powerful and effective." This verse emphasizes the communal aspect of prayer and its effectiveness in invoking divine authority for healing and supporting Christian community.

Through consistent prayer, we can grow to understand God's will and our ability to exercise the divine authority entrusted to us. As Ephesians 6:18 encourages, "And pray in the Spirit on all occasions with all kinds of prayers and requests. With this in mind, be alert and always keep on praying for all the Lord's people." This continuous engagement in prayer ensures that believers remain aligned with God's purposes and are empowered to act in His name.

Conclusion

Faith emerges as a potent weapon amidst the stringent complexities of spiritual warfare. It goes beyond mere belief and serves as an effective safeguard against myriad attacks by the devil. As we experience through the dense thicket of challenges thrown at us by evil powers, it is crucial to reinforce our belief in higher power. Our faith in God's all-powerful and ever-present nature empowers us to persevere through the trials and tribulations that the dark forces try to impose upon us. This faith becomes a beacon of hope in pitch darkness, guiding our voyage into lurking shadows and protecting us from damnation.

When faced with the enticing allure of deception and falsehoods crafted by the devil, faith empowers us to resist and remain steadfast, grounded in the unwavering and enduring love for God. The apostle Paul states in Ephesians 6:16, "Above all, taking the shield of faith with which you will be able to quench all the fiery darts of the wicked one." Amidst a roaring tide of tribulations, faith reassures us of hope and victory against dark forces.

Consistent nurturing maintains the vitality of faith and revitalizes our dependence on God's promises and blessings. Hebrews 11:6 affirms, "But without faith it is impossible to please Him, for he who comes to God must believe that He is, and that He is a rewarder of those who diligently seek Him." In our battle against the devil, our faith remains our best ally; it rises above the dark lies and fallacies to proclaim conquest and deliverance in God's omniscience. Let us fortify and place our full dependence on faith, a record of victory.

Chapter 6

Forward March!

> *"The righteous keep moving forward, and those with clean hands become stronger and stronger."*
> ***Job 17:9***

As we reach the conclusion of our journey through this book, we turn our focus to the ultimate call for every believer: to march forward in faith and determination against our enemy through spiritual warfare. This final chapter, "Forward March!" encapsulates the essence of our spiritual journey, urging us to press on with an unwavering resolve.

In the previous chapters, we explored the cosmic conflict between Jesus and His angels and Satan and his agents. Unlike the contemporary generic understanding of spiritual warfare, which often focuses on demonization and external demonic activities, this book seeks to expose demonic activities within us. It is within our hearts and minds that the devil wages his most insidious battles, tempting us to stray from the presence of God to sin against His law and to align ourselves, knowingly or unknowingly, with the forces of darkness.

The devil was relentless in his efforts to lead us away from God. He tempts us with the allurements of the world, desires of the flesh, and pride of life. He whispers doubts into our minds, sows discord among us, and seeks to weaken faith. But we are not without hope. Throughout this book, we have explored how to equip ourselves against the devil, stand firm in our faith, and empower ourselves spiritually.

In this concluding chapter, I employ the analogy of a soldier to emphasize God's mission and the indomitable bravery necessary to fulfill it while we are on Earth. Just as a soldier must be disciplined, vigilant, and prepared for battle, so too must we be in our spiritual lives. We engage in a cosmic conflict between good and evil, and the stakes are nothing less than our eternal lives.

If we desire to live eternally in tranquility, joy, and bliss, we must choose to be on God's side who loves us unconditionally. Conversely, the devil, who hates us and everything about God, aims to consume and humiliate us. To achieve this, he employs various temptations and worldly allurements to divert us from the path of righteousness and to distance us from God. Consequently, we must maintain our focus, faith, and reliance on scripture and God's spirit to wage war against the devil and his angels.

Our purpose is clear: to serve God and our fellow humans tirelessly until His victory, achieved on the cross of Calvary, ceasing all demonic activities forever. This service is not just a duty, but a joyous response to the salvation we receive from our Lord. As we march on, we are reminded of the strength and support we have in God, who helps us fulfill our destiny.

This final chapter encourages us to fortify our faith and embrace our role as soldiers of Christ. Let the truths and promises we have explored inspire us to march forward with confidence, knowing that faith is our greatest weapon and the most profound source of victory. Together, we move forward, guided by the light of the gospel and the love of our Savior, Jesus Christ, defeating the dark angels in Christ Jesus' holy name. Here is a song of encouragement.

1

Forward March, Christian Soldier!
Marching to the beat of our God-given drums,
We will follow Him anywhere and everywhere.
Our faith is unshakeable, and we will not waver.

Chorus

For He is our salvation, and He is our guide.
He has called us to be His soldiers,
And we will gladly respond.
We will stand up for what is right,
And we will never back down.

2

Our purpose is to serve Him and others,
And we will never stop until He is victorious.
May God be with you on your march,
And may He help you to fulfil your destiny.

Chorus

For He is our salvation, and He is our guide.
He has called us to be His soldiers,
And we will gladly respond.
We will stand up for what is right,
And we will never back down.

Bridge

In His name, Amen.
We march on with faith,
In His name, Amen.
We conquer through His grace.

Chorus

For He is our salvation, and He is our guide.
He has called us to be His soldiers,
And we will gladly respond.
We will stand up for what is right,
And we will never back down.

The Call to Arms

The book of Job states, "The righteous keep moving forward, and those with clean hands become stronger and stronger" (Job 17:9). As believers, we are called to be soldiers in the army of the Lord. This metaphor is not just a poetic expression but a powerful illustration of the spiritual realities we face. Just as a soldier must be disciplined, vigilant, and prepared for battle, so too must we be in our spiritual lives. We must be prepared to combat this devil through spiritual warfare. Our journey through this book has prepared us for this very moment to take up spiritual armor and stand firm against the forces of darkness.

A call to the arms is a call for action. It is a call to stand up to what is right, defend our faith, and protect those who are vulnerable. It is a call to be vigilant, aware of the enemy's tactics, and prepared to resist his advances. In this cosmic conflict, we are not left to fight alone. We have been given the Holy Spirit as a guide and helper. The Spirit empowers us to live out our faith with courage and conviction. He strengthens us when we are weak, gives us wisdom when we are confused and fills us with hope when we are discouraged.

As we don spiritual armor in Ephesians 6:10-18, we must also cultivate the qualities of a good soldier: discipline, perseverance, and courage. Discipline in our spiritual practices—prayer, scripture reading, worship, and fellowship— makes us spiritually fit and ready for battle. Perseverance enables us to endure hardships and setbacks without losing our hearts. Courage gives us the boldness to stand firm in faith, even in the face of opposition and persecution.

The battlefield is vast, and the stakes are high, but we are not without hope. We have been given everything we need for life and godliness through our knowledge of Him, who called us by His own glory and goodness (2 Pet 1:3). As we answer the call to arms, we do so with confidence that comes from knowing that our victory is already secured in Christ. He has triumphed over the powers of darkness through His death and resurrection, and we share this in His victory.

The Battle Within

The battle we face is not just against external forces but also within ourselves. The greatest struggle often occurs with the hidden recesses of our hearts and minds. In this internal conflict, the enemy seeks to gain a foothold by exploiting our weaknesses and vulnerabilities. To march forward effectively, we must understand and address the battles within us.

The apostle Paul, in his letter to the Romans, describes this inner struggle vividly: "For I do not do the good I want to do, but the evil I do not want to do—this I keep on doing. Now if I do what I do not want to do, it is no longer I who do it, but it is sin living in me that does it" (Rom 7:19-20). Paul acknowledges the tension between his desire to do good and the reality of sin at work within him. This struggle is common to all believers.

Sin is a powerful force that resides within our fallen nature. This corrupts our desires, distorts our thinking, and leads us away from God. The devil exploits this inclination towards sin, tempting us with what seems desirable but ultimately leading to destruction. He knows of our weaknesses and uses them against us, creating doubts, fears, and sinful desires.

To overcome the battle, we must first recognize the need for God's grace. We cannot defeat sin on our own. We can gain victory only through the power of the Holy Spirit. The Spirit works within us to transform our hearts and minds, renew our desires, and align them with God's will. This sanctification process is ongoing, requiring daily surrender and reliance on God's strength.

Self-examination is one of the most effective strategies for addressing a battle. Regularly examining thoughts, attitudes, and actions helps us identify areas that are susceptible to sin. Through prayerful reflection and confession, we bring these areas into light of God's truth. Confession is a powerful act that breaks the hold of sin and opens the door to God's healing and restoration. By keeping God's word in our hearts, we equip ourselves with truth that can counteract the lies of the enemy. When tempted, we recall specific verses that remind us of God's promises and commandments.

This practice strengthens our resolve and helps us resist the allure of sin. Accountability is also crucial in battles within us. Sharing our struggles with trusted fellow believers (often the hardest thing to do) provides both support and encouragement. They can offer wise counsel, pray to us, and help us stay on the right path. Accountability partners can challenge us to grow in our faith and hold us to commitments we have made to God.

Renewing one's minds is an ongoing process that requires intentional effort. We must be diligent in filling our minds with things that are true, noble, right, pure, lovely, and admirable (Phil 4:8). This means being selective regarding what we watch, read, and listen to. By focusing on positive and godly influences, we can cultivate a mindset conducive to spiritual growth and victory.

The battle within is also fought through worship and gratitude. When we worship, we shift our focus from struggles to God's greatness. Worship reminds us of His power, faithfulness, and love. It lifts our spirit and strengthens our faith. On the other hand, gratitude helps us recognize God's blessings in our lives. By cultivating a heart of thankfulness, we combat the negativity and discontentment that the enemy tries to instill in us.

Finally, we must remain vigilant in guarding our hearts. Proverbs 4:23 advises, "Above all else, guard your heart, for everything you do flows from it." This means being mindful of the influences we allow in our lives and setting boundaries to protect our spiritual wellbeing. It involves making conscious choices to avoid situations, relationships, or activities that could lead to temptation.

The battle is a significant aspect of our spiritual journey. It requires humility, honesty, and deep reliance on God's grace. As we confront our inner struggles, we grow stronger in faith and are more resilient against the enemy's attacks. By addressing the battle within, we are better equipped to march forward in larger cosmic conflicts.

The Cosmic Conflict

At the beginning of this book, we explored the cosmic conflict between Jesus and His angels, and Satan and his angels. This battle is not merely a myth or allegory, but a profound reality that affects every aspect of our lives. Understanding the nature of this conflict is crucial as we prepare to march forward. The Bible portrays this cosmic conflict as a battle between the Kingdom of God and the Kingdom of Darkness. Jesus described Satan as the "ruler of this world" (Jn 12:31) who has been given temporary authority over the earth. This authority was usurped through the fall of humanity when Adam and Eve disobeyed God and aligned themselves with the serpent's deception. Since then, Satan sought to establish his dominion by leading people away from God and into sin.

However, God's redemption planwas set in motion from the beginning. Through the life, death, and resurrection of Jesus Christ, Satan's power was decisively defeated. Jesus' victory on the cross disarmed the powers and authorities of darkness, making a public spectacle of them and triumphing over them by the cross (Col 2:15). This victory is the foundation of our hopes and the basis for our confidence in spiritual warfare. While ultimate victory has been secured, the battle continues until the final consummation of God's kingdom. We live in the tension of the "already but not yet," where the kingdom of God has been inaugurated, but not fully realized. Although defeated, Satan still seeks to undermine God's purposes and destroy His people. This ongoing conflict manifests in various ways including spiritual oppression, moral decay, and systemic evil.

Understanding this cosmic conflict helps us to recognize the broader context of our personal struggles. Our battle against sin, temptation, and demonic influence is part of a larger war that spans both the visible and invisible realms. It is a struggle between the forces of light and darkness, truth and deception, life and death. In this conflict, we are called to be active participants rather than passive observers. Our role is to advance God's kingdom by living our faith, proclaiming the gospel, and demonstrating His love and justice. This involves both personal and societal transformations. We are agents of change, bringing light into dark places, and hopelessness.

This cosmic conflict also highlights the importance of spiritual discernment. The enemy is cunning and deceptive, often masquerading as an angel of light (2 Cor 11:14). He sows confusion, division, and false teachings to lead people astray. As believers, we must be grounded in the truth of God's word and be sensitive to the leading of the Holy Spirit. Discernment helps us recognize the enemy's schemes and stand firm in truth.

Moreover, cosmic conflict underscores the necessity of spiritual unity. Jesus prayed for His followers to be one, as He and the Father are one (Jn 17:21). Unity among believers is a powerful testimony to the world and a formidable defense against the enemy's attacks. By fostering a spirit of unity, we strengthen our collective witnesses and create a supportive community that can withstand spiritual opposition.

Our engagement with this cosmic conflict is also marked by hope. We are assured of the ultimate victory of God's Kingdom. The book of Revelation provides a glimpse of the final outcome, where Satan and his forces are defeated and cast into a lake of fire, and God's people reign with Him in a new heaven and a new earth. This hope gives us the courage to persevere and the perspective of enduring hardship.

As we march forward in this cosmic conflict, we do so with assurance that we are on the winning side. Jesus, our commander-in-chief, leads us with wisdom, power, and love. He equips us with everything that we need to stand firm and advance His kingdom. By staying close to Him, we can find the strength to overcome and the grace to endure. The cosmic conflict is both a sobering reality and exhilarating adventure. This calls for a higher purpose and deeper commitment. As we engage in this battle, we fulfill our destiny as God's children and contribute to His redemptive work in the world.

Pressing Onward

We are called on to press forward with unwavering resolutions. "Not that I have already obtained all this, or have already arrived at my goal, but I press on to take hold of that for which Christ Jesus took hold of me" (Phil 3:12). The journey of faith is not a sprint, but a marathon, requiring endurance, perseverance, and steadfast focus on our ultimate goal. Paul's word to the

Philippians encapsulate this mindset: pressing on to take hold of the prize for which Christ has called us.

Christian life is characterized by continuous growth and transformation. Each day, it presents new challenges and opportunities to deepen our faith and become more like Christ. This process, often referred to as sanctification, is the work of the Holy Spirit, shaping us into the image of Jesus. This journey requires intentionality and commitment.

Pressing onward involves maintaining a forward perspective. Paul speaks of forgetting what is behind and straining toward what is ahead (Phil 3:13). This does not mean ignoring our past, but rather not being held back by it. We learn from our experiences, both successes and failures, but we do not let them define or limit ourselves. Instead, we keep our eyes fixed on Jesus, the author and the perfecter of our faith, and the prize awaiting us.

One of the keys to pressing is to cultivate resilience. onward Resilience is the ability to bounce back from setbacks and keep going despite difficulties. It is rooted in the assurance that God is with us and that His grace is sufficient for every challenge that we face. Resilience is built through trust in God's promises, a supportive faith community, and disciplined spiritual life.

Another aspect of pressing onward is embracing our calling and mission. Each believer has been uniquely gifted and called to contribute to God's kingdom. Discovering and fulfilling this call brings a sense of purpose and direction to our lives. It involves using our talent, time, and resources to serve others, advance the gospel, and bring glory to God. When we are engaged in our mission, we find joy, fulfillment, and purpose, and even amid challenges.

The community plays a crucial role in our journey to the pressing onward. We are not meant to walk along this path alone. The body of Christ (the Church) is a source of strength, encouragement, and accountability. Through relationships with other believers, we find support in times of need, and celebration in times of victory. Community helps us stay focused and motivated, reminding us that we are part of something larger than ourselves.

Pressing onward is a call to live with a purpose, resilience, and hope. It is an invitation to journey deeper into our faith, grow in Christlikeness, and contribute to God's redemptive work. As we march forward, let us do so with confidence, knowing that we are not alone and that God is with us every step in the way. Together, we can face the challenges ahead, overcome the obstacles in our path, and press on the prize that awaits us.

Marching Forward in Faith

As we press onward, we are called on to march forward in faith. Faith is the foundation of our spiritual journey, and the lens through which we see and understand the world. It is the assurance of things hoped for and the conviction of things not seen (Heb 11:1). Our faith in God propels us forward, giving us courage to face the unknown and the strength to overcome obstacles.

Marching forward in faith requires trust in God's character and promises. Throughout the scripture, we see countless examples of God's faithfulness to His people. From the deliverance of Israelites from Egypt to the resurrection of Jesus Christ, God has consistently demonstrated His power and love. These stories remind us that we can trust God to lead us, provide for us, and fulfill His promises.

One of the most inspiring examples of faith in action is Abraham's story. God called Abraham to leave his homeland and go to a place that He would show him. Despite not knowing where he was going, Abraham obeyed and embarked on a journey of faith. His trust in God was so profound that he was willing to sacrifice his son Isaac, believing that God could raise him from the dead (Heb 11:17-19). Abraham's faith was credited to him as righteousness, and he became known as the father of faith.

Like Abraham, we are called to step out in faith, even when the path ahead is uncertain. This may involve making difficult decisions, taking risks, or facing insurmountable challenges. Faith requires us to let go of our fears and doubts and place our trust in God's sovereignty and goodness. It is a daily choice to believe that God is who He says He is and that He will do what He has promised.

Faith is also about seeing beyond the current circumstances. It is easy to be discouraged when we encounter trials and setbacks. However, faith enables us to see God's hand at work, even during adversity. It reminds us that our present difficulties are temporary and that God is using them to shape us and prepare us for something greater. Faith gives us the perspective of enduring and hoping to continue moving forward.

Marching forward in faith involves a dynamic relationship with God. It is not a one-time decision, but an ongoing journey of growth and discovery. As we spend time in God's word, prayers, and fellowships with other believers, our faith is strengthened. We begin to see God's purposes and plans for our lives more clearly. Our trust in Him deepens, and we become more attuned to His voice and leadership.

As we march forward in faith, we must also cultivate a spirit of gratitude. Gratitude shifts our focus from what we lack to what we have been given. This reminds us of God's goodness and faithfulness in our lives. By practicing gratitude, we develop a positive and hopeful outlook that fuels faith and resilience. This enables us to see God's blessings amid challenges and to trust that He is working all things for our good.

Ultimately, marching forward in faith is about aligning our lives with God's purpose and trusting Him to guide us. It is a journey that requires courage, commitment, and deep reliance on God's grace. As we move forward, let us do so with confidence, knowing that our faith is our greatest weapon and most profound source of victory. Together, we march forward, guided by the light of the gospel and love of our Savior, Jesus Christ.

The Victory Ahead

The journey of faith is filled with challenges but is also marked by the promise of victory. As we press onward and march forward in faith, we do so with the assurance that victory is both possible and guaranteed. This victory is rooted in the triumph of Jesus Christ over sin, death, and powers of darkness.

The ultimate victory was secured on the cross. When Jesus died and rose again, He defeated the devil and all of his schemes. His resurrection is the foundation of our hope and assurance of salvation. Because of Jesus' victory, we can face the future with confidence, knowing that nothing can separate us from the love of God (Rom 8:38-39).

The promise of victory is a source of strength and encouragement as we navigate the challenges of life. It reminds us that no matter how difficult the battle is, we are fighting from a place of victory. The enemy may try to discourage and defeat us, but we stand firm in the knowledge that he has already been defeated. Our role is to enforce the victory that Christ has won, living out of our faith with boldness and perseverance.

Victory in Christ is not just a future hope; it is also a present reality. As we abide by Him and walk in obedience to His commands, we experience His victory in our daily lives. This victory manifests in various ways: overcoming sin; finding peace during turmoil; experiencing healing and restoration; and seeing God's provision and guidance. Each victory we experience is a testament to God's faithfulness and foretaste of the ultimate victory that awaits us. These victories are the testimony to God's everlasting protection and guidance.

The book of Revelation provides a powerful glimpse of this ultimate victory. It describes Satan's final defeat and the establishment of God's eternal kingdom. In Revelation 21:4, we are given a beautiful promise: "He will wipe every tear from their eyes. There will be no more death or mourning or crying or pain, for the old order of things has passed away." This vision of the future fills us with hope and inspires us to persevere, knowing that our present suffering is not worth comparing with the glory that will be revealed in us (Rom 8:18).

As we look forward to this victory, we are called upon to live with a sense of urgency and purpose. Our time on Earth is limited, and we have been given a mission to fulfill. We are ambassadors of Christ, called upon to share the good news of His victory with the world. This mission requires us to be proactive and intentional, seeking opportunities to serve, love, and witnesses.

Living in light of victory also means walking in freedom. Jesus came to set us free from the bondage of sin and fear. As we embrace His victory, we are liberated to live as children of God, free to pursue our calling, and to boldly live out our faith. This freedom is not a license to live as we please, but an invitation to live as we ought, reflecting God's love and grace in all that we do.

The victory ahead is both encouragement and challenge. It encourages us by reminding us that our efforts are not in vain, and that God is with us every step of the way. It challenges us to live in a manner worthy of our calling, to stay focused on our mission, and to keep our eyes fixed on Jesus, the pioneer and perfecter of our faith (Hebrews 12:2).

Living out Victory

As we embrace the promise of victory, the question arises: How do we live out this victory in our daily lives? Living out victory involves more than just acknowledging it; it requires us to embody it in our actions, attitudes, and relationships. It is about allowing Christ's victory to shape and transform every aspect of our lives.

Living out victory begins with a transformed mindset. Romans 12:2 urges us not to conform to the pattern of this world, but to be transformed by the renewing of our minds. This transformation is crucial because our thoughts influence our actions. By filling our minds with God's truth and aligning our thinking with His word, we begin to see ourselves and the world from His perspective. This renewed mindset empowers us to make decisions that reflect faith and respond to life's challenges with grace and wisdom.

Another key aspect of living out victory is walking in love. Jesus commanded us to love one another as He has loved us (Jn 13:34). This love is not just an emotion but an action. It involves serving others, showing kindness and compassion, and putting the needs of others before our own needs. When we walk in love, we demonstrate the reality of Christ's victory in our lives and reflect His character on those around us.

Living out victory also means walking in holiness. We are called to be holy because God is holy (1 Pet 1:16). Holiness involves setting ourselves apart for God's purposes and living in a way that honors Him. This means avoiding sin and pursuing righteousness. This pursuit of holiness is not about striving for perfection in our strength but about allowing the Holy Spirit to work in us, transforming us from inside out.

Another important aspect of living out victory is cultivating a heart of gratitude. Gratitude shifts our focus from what we lack to what we have been given. This reminds us of God's goodness and faithfulness in our lives. By practicing gratitude, we develop a positive and hopeful outlook that fuels faith and resilience. This enables us to see God's blessings amid challenges and to trust that He is working all things for our good.

Living out victory also requires us to be witnesses to Christ's love and truth. Jesus commissioned us to go and make disciples of all nations (Matt 28:19). Sharing the gospel is an essential part of living a victorious life. It involves proclaiming good news of Jesus' death and resurrection, testifying to what He has done in our lives, and inviting others to experience His salvation. Our words and actions consistently point to Christ and hope that we have in Him.

A New Creation through Christ

The gospel of Jesus Christ brings a transformative message for us to become a new creation. By coming to Christ, we are adopted into God's family, forgiven our sins, and empowered with a Christ-like character. This profound change offers us an eternal life through the faith in Jesus. We are called to live for God in this world, embracing our identity as a new creation by following Christ and obeying His commands.

Believers are called to holiness, living solely for God. With His power, we can overcome any challenge, becoming more like Jesus in every aspect. Following Him, He guides us and helps us grow in our relationship with Him. This transformation manifests in our lives through joy and peace when we obey God's command. We become people God desires us to be filled with compassion and driven to help others. Our decisions are based on what is best for spiritual growth, not what is easiest or most comfortable. We remain grateful for God's blessings, even in difficult times, living to glorify Him and share His love.

The gospel is a message of hope, offering an eternal life through faith in Christ. This hope is true and available. When faced with these challenges, we can rely on God's power through Christ. The gospel also brings peace, guiding our steps and helping us overcome the traps of the devil. It offers joy, knowing that we are forgiven, and has access to God's life-giving power. Through the gospel, we learn to live for God, enjoying His blessings now and in the future, promised by Christ. This good news is for everyone who believes in Jesus Christ and receives His transformative grace.

All people are created in the image of God and have access to eternal life through faith in Jesus Christ. This gospel brings hope, peace, and joy to people. Hope is based on our salvation in Christ and is always available. Peace comes from relying on God's power to overcome these difficulties. Joy comes from knowing that we are forgiven and connected to God's life-giving power. As we follow Jesus, He guides us, helping us grow in our relationship with Him and experiencing new creations in every area of our lives.

Not Past, but Future in Christ

In Christ, we are not defined by our past, but by our future. Our future is not a distant, unfamiliar place; it is our current reality. We live in the future, not the past, which means that we can live faithfully in the present while looking forward to the future God has planned for us. This perspective allows us to enjoy today while eagerly anticipating tomorrow and all God has in store for us.

When we focus on what is possible and look forward to the future, we avoid dwelling on past events or potential negative outcomes. Instead, we concentrate on the possibility that God presents us with. This mindset enables us to appreciate today regardless of our circumstances.

The apostle Paul discusses this concept in Romans 8:18-25. He explained that God created us to enjoy life and eternal joy. He assures us that God will always protect us and keep us safe. Essentially, everything that happens in life provides an opportunity for us to learn and grow. Although we cannot control every event, we can control our responses. We can choose to find joy in life and trust that God will protect us. This perspective helps us to live fully in the present and look forward to the future with hope and anticipation.

Living in Christ focuses on the future. We can rest assured that everything will work out for our good, trusting God to take care of us and provide the happiness and success we need. By focusing on the present moment and living according to God's plan, we can enjoy it today and prepare for tomorrow with hope and anticipation.

Faith for the future is essential to living faithfully in present. We must believe in God's goodness and His promises to us. By trusting God, we also trust ourselves and our ability to follow His guidance. Although we cannot control everything that occurs, we can control our reactions. By living according to God's plan, we can find joy in the present and look forward to the future with hope and anticipation, knowing that God is always with us and will care for us.

We have the choice to enjoy life and find joy, even in difficult times. Trusting that God will always protect us allows us to live fully in the present and look forward to the future with hope. Pray that we may live faithfully today; trusting the future God has planned for us.

The Bible teaches that everything is possible for those who believe (Mk 9:23). Let us have faith in God's promises in our lives. Believe in his plan and trust him to carry it out.

Cleansing with the Blood of Christ

We believe that Christ's blood is the ultimate remedy for sin and physical healing. Jesus Himself said, "If you forgive men their trespasses, your heavenly Father will also forgive you" (Matthew 6:14). This divine forgiveness acts as cleansing from all our sins, enabling us to forgive others as well. We must invite Jesus into our hearts and pray to Him for healing and forgiveness.

If you experience physical symptoms that seem related to sin, consider speaking with your church pastor (only if you can trust them) who can help you explore your spiritual side. Understanding our sinful nature and damage caused by sin is crucial. A trained pastor, counselor, or spiritual person can support you as you work to overcome these issues.

The blood of Christ cleanses us from sin, prayer, and repentance, which are also essential for healing. I encourage you to pray for guidance, physical healing, if needed, spiritual healing, and forgiveness. The Bible mentions physical healing, such as when Jesus healed a man who was paralyzed for 18 years. Jesus emphasized the importance of spiritual nourishment by saying, "Unless you eat the flesh of the Son of Man and drink His blood, you have no life in you. Whoever eats My flesh and drinks My blood has eternal life, and I will raise him up at the last day" (Jn 6:55-57). Physical healing often signifies acceptance of Jesus as Savior, as seen when Jesus healed a woman with a bleeding issue, and the crowd marveled at His power (Matthew 9:34).

Physical healing is evident throughout the scripture. Paul, for example, spoke of his own healing: "And my flesh was restored like the flesh of a child, and I felt much joy" (2 Cor 12:7). This is a physical manifestation of God's healing power. Physical healing is a sign of God's grace, confirming His presence in our lives and reminding us that we are not alone in our struggle. I encourage you to join prayer groups and ministries focused on physical healing for fellowships and support. However, physical healing is not always guaranteed. Sometimes, symptoms persist or worsen; therefore, it is important to seek medical help if they experience severe symptoms. Nevertheless, let us not forget the supreme sacrifice of Jesus Christ and the power of His blood. Through Christ's shed blood, we experience forgiveness, cleansing from sin, and physical healing. This experience empowers us in our spiritual lives to embrace God's love and law, uniting Him against the devil in spiritual warfare.

Running the Christian Race

Embarking on the journey of Christian faith can seem daunting, yet it is one of the most rewarding endeavors you will ever undertake. Imagine your life as a race that requires dedication, perseverance, and faith. This race is not about speed but about endurance, and it is one where every step brings you closer to a deeper relationship with God.

To begin, immerse in scriptures. The Bible is our spiritual roadmap filled with guidance, wisdom, and encouragement for this race. Start by reading a few chapters each day, or even a few verses. Let these words sink into your heart and mind, providing the spiritual nourishment you need.

Identifying a community of fellow believers is also crucial. There is strength in numbers, and joining a local church can connect you with others on the same journey. Together, you can support and encourage each other, making the path less solitary and fulfilling.

Prayers are the lifeline of this race. This is your direct line of communication with God. Make it a daily habit to talk to Him, asking for guidance, strength, and endurance. This spiritual discipline will help you grow in faith and keep you grounded.

Regularly attending church services is another key aspect. It is a place where one can learn more about the gospel, worship together, and participate in ministries that can help one grow spiritually. The communal worship experience strengthens the resolution and enriches faith.

Serving others is a tangible way of living one's faith. Acts of kindness and generosity, whether large or small, reflect Christ's love and compassion. Helping someone with a chore, offering a kind word, or volunteering your time are ways to actively practice their faith.

Temptation is a reality faced by every Christian. Remember that Jesus was tempted in every way but remained sinless. By following His example and relying on His strength, you can overcome any obstacle that Satan throws your way. Stay vigilant and grounded in your faith.

Seeking a mentor is incredibly beneficial. Someone who has walked the path before you and has the wisdom to share can provide invaluable guidance and support. They can help navigate the challenges and keep you motivated.

Believing about oneself is essential. With God's help, anything is made possible. When times get tough, remember that you are not running this race alone. God is with you in every step of the way, offering His strength and guidance.

Perseverance is key. No matter how difficult the journey may seem, do not give up on your faith or the goal of becoming more Christ-like. Jesus promises to be with you always, providing comfort and strength.

Keep moving forward! You have everything that you need to run this race with endurance and faith. Trust in God's promises, seek His guidance, and stay connected to the community of believers. Together, we can overcome any challenges and continue to grow faithfully.

In this race, there will be moments of struggle and triumph. Each step you take is closer to the ultimate goal—eternal life with Christ. So, lace up your spiritual running shoes, fix your eyes on Jesus, and run the race marked out for you with perseverance.

Keep Going Forward, Christian Soldier!

We all face tough times and moments when we feel like giving up. But we cannot. We must keep moving forward by remembering that we are never alone. God is always by our side guiding us through every challenge. With courage and faith, we can face anything that comes our way and never abandon our dreams and goals.

So, Christian soldier, press on! You can do it! One way to keep going is to consistently do what is right and good, even when it seems like no one is listening. Together, we can inspire and motivate one another to continue pushing through difficult times. Be encouraged, Christian soldier! You can accomplish anything you have set your mind to! Remember: God is always with you. Whether you feel down about the state of the world or just need a bit of encouragement, God is there to help you. Keep moving forward, knowing that God has your back!

Trust God

In a world filled with challenges and uncertainties, we often find ourselves overwhelmed by the enormous number of problems that seem beyond our control. However, it is crucial to note that we are not expected to fix everything on our own. Instead, we can place our trust in God, who has consistently proven His faithfulness throughout history. Trusting God means believing in His promises and relying on His guidance, even when we cannot see the way forward.

God's faithfulness is a central theme in the Bible and provides a solid foundation for faith. He assures us in Isaiah 41:10, "Fear not, for I am with you; be not dismayed, for I am your God; I will strengthen you, I will help you, I will uphold you with my righteous right hand." This powerful scripture reminds us that God is always present, ready to support, and strengthen us in times of need.

By trusting God, we acknowledge that He is in control and has a plan for our lives. This trust allows us to surrender our worries and anxieties to Him, knowing that He will work everything for our good. This does not mean that we will never face difficulties but assures us that we will never face them alone. God's presence is a constant source of comfort and strength, helping us navigate life's storms with confidence and peace.

Cry Out to God

When life becomes overwhelming and we find ourselves struggling to cope, it is essential to remember that we have a direct line of communication with God. Crying out to God in times of trouble is not a sign of weakness, but a testament to our faith in His power to help us. The Bible is filled with examples of people who turned to God in their darkest moments and found solace and strength in His presence. These stories serve as reminders that we are not alone in our struggles. Others face similar challenges and have emerged victorious through their unwavering faith in God. In times of distress, prayer becomes a lifeline. It is a way to express our deepest fears, hopes, and desires toward God, trusting that He hears us and will respond.

Crying out to God not only brings comfort, but also reminds us of our dependence on Him. It shifts our focus from limitations to His limitless power and love. Through prayer, we can find peace amid chaos and hope in the face of despair. By turning to God, we allow His presence to fill our hearts and minds, giving us courage to face any challenge with confidence.

Jesus Christ is Our Motivation

Christians are called to walk in faith, continually pressing towards the goals that God has set before us. This forward march is about spiritual progress, involving growth in our relationship with Christ, deepening our understanding of His teachings, and striving to live out His example daily.

By putting our faith in Christ, He provides the strength needed to face challenges. He is our ultimate source of motivation, guiding us throughout life's journey. Living according to His teachings enables us to move forward with confidence and hope, regardless of the obstacles in our path.

To lead a strong and successful Christian life, our motivation comes from Jesus Christ. Trusting in Him ensures that we receive guidance and strength to overcome any difficulties. He helps us stay focused on our goals and leads the fight between sin and evil. Following Christ allows us to grow in character and knowledge, thus becoming examples of others.

In times of weakness, He is our strength, in despair, our hope, and in uncertainty, our guide. As we continue our Christian Walk, we do so with the assurance that Christ is with us, leading us toward victory.

Move Forward!

Understanding the importance of moving forward and setting goals is crucial for achieving success. There are four key reasons why setting goals is essential.

1. **Staying Motivated**: Without clear goals, it can be challenging to maintain motivation. Goals provide you with a target to aim for and help you stay focused on your objectives. When you have a clear plan for what you want to achieve, it becomes much easier to stay on track.
2. **Preventing Stagnation**: Without forward movement, you risk becoming stagnant. Stagnation can occur when one's goals are too small or when one loses focus on what is important. This loss of direction can lead to a decrease in motivation and performance. By setting and focusing on goals, stagnation can be avoided and continued to progress.
3. **Encouraging risk taking**: Having specific goals makes it easier to take risks. When a new opportunity arises, knowing exactly what you are aiming to achieve gives you the confidence to pursue it. Clear goals make one more likely to take the risks necessary to achieve success.
4. **Seeing Quick Results**: Setting goals often leads to visible results quickly. When you work towards a specific purpose, you can usually see your progress, which can be highly motivating. Seeing the fruits of your labor encourages you to keep moving forward.

In summary, setting goals is vital for achieving success. It helps one stay motivated, prevents stagnation, encourages risk-taking, and allows one to see progress quickly. By understanding and implementing goal setting, you can effectively move forward in your life and achieve the desired outcomes.

Conclusion

Finally, it is crucial for everyone who claims to be Christian to acknowledge the cosmic battle between good and evil. This spiritual warfare is not just a metaphor, but a real and ongoing struggle that affects every aspect of our lives. We must remain on the side of God, standing firm against the devil and fighting the good fight of faith.

Throughout this book, we journeyed together through the Bible, uncovering the devil's evil plots and learning how to combat his influence through spiritual warfare. We explored the significance of recognizing our own inner demons and understanding their subtle yet powerful impact on our lives. By doing so, we have equipped ourselves with the knowledge and tools necessary to resist these unholy influences and to reclaim spiritual strength.

Christians are called vigilant and steadfast, like soldiers prepared for battle. The Apostle Peter's exhortation in 1 Peter 5:8-9 reminds us to "be sober-minded; be watchful. Your adversary, the devil prowls around like a roaring lion, seeking someone to devour. Resist him, firm in your faith, knowing that the same kinds of suffering are being experienced by your brotherhood throughout the world." This call for vigilance and resistance is the cornerstone of spiritual defense.

Our spiritual armor, described in Ephesians 6:10-18 represents a vital aspect of our faith and relationship with God. By putting on this armor daily, we can stand strong against the devil schemes and protect ourselves from his attacks.

However, our battle does not end with personal defense. We are also called to advance to forward march against evil in our lives, within us, and then in the world around us. This means actively seeking to overcome weaknesses, addressing the sins and temptations that hold us back, and striving to live lives that reflect God's love and truth. It also means being a beacon of light in a dark world, sharing a message of hope and salvation with those around us.

In this controversy, unity and solidarity among believers are crucial. We are not alone in this battle; we are part of a global brotherhood that experiences similar struggles. By supporting and encouraging one another, we can strengthen our collective resolve and enhance our ability to resist the devil's deception.

"Dealing with Your Demons" is a call to action for every Christian. It is a reminder that spiritual warfare is a daily reality, and that we must be proactive in our faith. By setting clear goals, staying motivated, preventing stagnation, encouraging risk-taking, and celebrating victories, we can overcome the unholy influences in our lives and emerge victorious in this cosmic battle.

In conclusion, let us remember that Christ assures our ultimate victory. As we stand firm in our faith, equipped with the armor of God, and united with our fellow believers, we can confidently face challenges ahead. Let us march forward, resolute, and unwavering, determined to defeat evil forces and bring glory to God's name.

Bibliography

Arnold, Clinton E. 1997. *3 Crucial Questions about Spiritual Warfare.* Grand Rapids, MI: Baker Academic.

________. 2009. *Power of Darkness: Principalities & Powers in Paul's Letters.* Downers Grove, IL: InterVarsity Press.

Basharin, Pavel. "Sacred Wars" in the Field of Muslim Demonology" *Journal for Studies of Islam and Muslim Societies.* Vol. 2, No. 2. DOI: http://dx.doi.org/10.24848/islmlg.02.2.02.

Bhattacharyya, N.N. 2000. *Indian Demonology: The Inverted Pantheon.* Delhi, India: Manohar Publishers & Distributors

Bonhoeffer, Dietrich. 1954. *Life Together.* London, UK: SCM Press.

Boyd, Greg. 2008. "What Is the Warfare Worldview?" *ReKnew.* January 15. https://reknew.org/2008/01/intro-to-warfare-worldview/.

Boyd, Gregory A. 1997. *God at War: The Bible & Spiritual Conflict.* Downers Grove, IL: InterVarsity Press.

Bradfield, Bill. 2012. *On Reading the Bible: Thoughts and Reflections of Over 500 Men and Women, from St. Augustine to Oprah Winfrey.* Mineola, NY: Dover Publications.

Butkiewicz, W. (2020, June 23). *Gluttony: How Esau lost his birthright to Jacob (deferred gratification as a predictor of success).* The Amplifier. https://www.theamplifier.org/post/gluttony-how-esau-lost-his-birthright-to-jacob-deferred-gratification-as-a-success-indicator

Coleman, Marc. 2015. "Ellen White on Confrontation with Evil Spiritual Powers," *Journal of Adventist Mission Studies*: Vol. 11: No. 2, 95-104

Dass, Rakesh Peter (2018) “Act Properly: Rāmānuja and Luther on Works,” Journal of Hindu-Christian Studies: Vol. 31, Article 21. Available at: https://doi.org/10.7825/2164-6279.1698

Doukhan, Jacques B. 2016. *Genesis: Seventh-day Adventist International Bible Commentary.* USA: Pacific Press Publishing and Review and Herald Publishing.

Editor’s choice (2019). *Theology Today,* 75(4), 504-509. https://doi.org/10.1177/0040573618805929

Ferguson, Everett. 2009. *Baptism in the Early Church: History, Theology, and Liturgy in the First Five Centuries.* Grand Rapids, MI: William B. Eerdmans Publishing Company.

Harman, M. (2016). “An Example of Hell from the Ottoman Miniature Art: Dragon-Shaped Hell in Ahvâl-I Qiyâmeh.” *The Journal of International Social Research,* Vol.9, Issue 3: 1065-1065.

Hesse, C. & Floyd, K. (2019). Affection substitution: The effect of pornography consumptiononcloserelationships.JournalofSocialandPersonalRelationships, 36(11-12), 3887-3907. https://doi.org/10.1177/0265407519841719

Hiebert, Paul G. 2001. *Anthropological Reflections on Missiological Issues.* Grand Rapids, MI: Baker Books.

________. 2008. *Transforming Worldviews an Anthropological Understanding of How People Change.* Grand Rapids, , MI: Baker Academic.

________. 2009. *The Gospel in Human Contexts: Anthropological Explorations for Contemporary Missions.* Grand Rapids, MI: Baker Academic.

Hughes, Selwyn. 2013. *Everyday with Jesus Daily Bible.* Nashville, TN: Holman Bible Publishers.

Ing, Richard. 1996. *Spiritual Warfare.* New Kensington, PA: Whitaker House.

Ingram, Chip. 2015. *The Invisible War: What Every Believer Needs to Know about Satan, Demons & Spiritual Warfare.* Grand Rapids, MI: Baker Books.

Kasmana, K., Sabana, S., Gunawan, I.D., & Ahmad, H.A. (2018). “The Belief in the Existence of Supernatural Beings in the Community of Moslem Sundanese.” *Journal of Arts and Humanities,* Vol. 7, Issue 4: 11-21. DOI: http://dx.doi.org/10.18533/journal.v7i4.1375

Kolic, Marko. 2009. "The Demonology of Ellen G. White" *Journal of Adventist Mission Studies.* Vol. 5, No. 2: 98-105. https://digitalcommons.andrews.edu/jams/vol5/iss2/11.

Kraft, Charles H. 2010. *Anthropology for Christian Witness.* Maryknoll, NY: Orbis Books.

________. 2012. *I Give You Authority: Practicing the Authority Jesus Gave Us.* Grand Rapids, MI: Chosen Books.

________. 2016. *Defeating Dark Angels: Breaking Demonic Oppression in the Believer's Life.* Grand Rapids, MI: Baker Books.

________. 2017. *Power Encounter in Spiritual Warfare.* Eugene, OR: Wipf and Stock Publishers.

Life, One Way Truth. 2019. "Being Spiritually Proactive Instead of Reactive.." *One Way Truth Life.* January 24, 2019. https://onewaytruthlife.com/2018/07/spiritually-proactive-vs-reactive/.

Mecca, Valerie. 2020. *Prayer: A spiritual weapon of mass destruction: Praying the books of ephesians, colossians, philemons, and philippians.* Amazon Kindle Edition.

Moreau, A. Scott. 2008. *Essentials of Spiritual Warfare: Equipped to Win the Battle.* Eugene, OR: WIPF & STOCK.

Naugle, David K. 2002. *Worldview: The History of a Concept.* Grand Rapids, MI: William B. Eerdmans Publishing Company.

Page, Sydney H.T. 1995. *Powers of Evil: A Biblical Study of Satan and Demons.* Grand Rapids, MI: Baker Books.

Payne, William P., 2018. *Adventures in Spiritual Warfare: Defeating Satan and Living a Victorious Life.* Eugene, OR: Wipf and Stock Publishers.

Peckham, John C., 2018. *Theodicy of Love: Cosmic Conflict and the Problem of Evil.* Grand Rapids, MI: Baker Academic.

Pertejo, E. M. and López, V. L. (2022). The demons of judas and mary magdalene in medieval art. Religions, 13(11), 1048. https://doi.org/10.3390/rel13111048

Piper, J. (2016). *Satan's ten strategies against you.* Desiring God. https://www.desiringgod.org/articles/satans-ten-strategies-against-you

Rek, S., Sheaves, B., & Freeman, D. (2017). "Nightmares in the general population: identifying potential causal factors." *Social psychiatry and psychiatric epidemiology*, 52(9), 1123–1133. https://doi.org/10.1007/s00127-017-1408-7

Rendell, Ruth. 2010. *The Epistle of Paul the Apostle to The Romans.* Edinburg, UK: Canongate Books.

Strickmann, Michael. 2002. *Chinese Magical Medicine.* Stanford, CA: Stanford University Press.

Swearingen, Shyann. 2021. "Spiritual Warfare: Definition, Viewpoints, and Why It Matters." *Just Disciple.* February 1. https://justdisciple.com/spiritual-warfare/.

Tamir, C., Connaughton, A., & Salazar, A. M. (2020, July 20). *The global god divide.* Pew Research Center. https://www.pewresearch.org/religion/2020/07/20/the-global-god-divide/#:~:text=And%20how%20important%20are%20God,moral%20and%20have%20good%20values

Texada, Greg. 2012. *Jesus Did It for You: Receiving Your Inheritance.* Bloomington, IN: WestBow Press.

Unger, Merrill F. 1994. *Biblical Demonology: A Study of Spiritual Forces at Work Today.* Grand Rapids, MI: Kregel Publications.

Wagner, C. Peter. 1997. *Praying with Power: How to Pray Effectively and Hear Clearly from God.* Shippensberg, PA: Destiny Image Publishers.

White, Ellen G. 1890. *Patriarchs and Prophets* (Washington D.C.: Review and Herald Publishing Association, 1999, 38.

Wilt, J. A., Grubbs, J. B., Exline, J. J. & Pargament, K. I. (2016) "Personality, Religious and Spiritual Struggles, and Well-Being" *Psychology of Religion and Spirituality*, 8(4): 341-351. http://dx.doi.org/10.1037/rel0000054

Wood, Tim. 2018. "10 Signs of Spiritual Attack." *Evergreen Valley Church.* Evergreen Valley Church. August 31. https://evcsj.org/blog/2018/8/31/10-signs-of-spiritual-attack.

APPENDICES

Appendix A

Prayer Logbook

This tool is designed to help deepen one's relationship with God through regular, intentional prayers. It guides you in documenting your personal and intercessory prayers, tracking your spiritual journey, and reflecting on God's faithfulness in answering the prayers.

Personal prayer logbook: Use this section to record your personal requests and needs.

Date	Request	Scripture Reference	Notes/Updates
	Your personal prayer request	Scripture that inspires you	Any updates or reflections

Personal prayer logbook: Use this section to note down the needs and requests of others that you are praying for.

Date	Name/Person	Request	Scripture Reference	Notes/Updates
			Scripture that inspires you	**Any updates or reflections**

Thanksgiving and Praise logbook: Record moments of gratitude and praise to God for His blessings and answers to prayers.

Date	Reasons for Thanksgiving/Praise	Scripture Reference	Notes/Reflection

Prayer Reflections and Answers: Reflect on how God has responded to your prayers.

Date	Original Request	God's Answer/ Response	Scripture Reference	Reflections and Gratitude

Appendix B

Spiritual Gifts Assessment

Creating a Spiritual Gifts Assessment can help individuals identify and understand their spiritual gifts, which can then be used for the betterment of their faith community. Below is a template you can use to create a comprehensive Spiritual Gifts Assessment in a Word document.

Spiritual Gifts Assessment

Read each statement and decide how well it describes you. Use the following scale to respond to each statement:

5 - Strongly Agree
4 - Agree
3 - Neutral
2 - Disagree
1 - Strongly Disagree

Write the number that corresponds to your response in the space provided.

Personal Information:

Name: ________________________________

Date: _________________________________

Assessment Statements:

#	Statement	Response (1-5)
1	I enjoy organizing and coordinating events or activities.	
2	I find it easy to share my faith with others.	
3	I often take time to listen to others and provide support and encouragement.	
4	I feel called to help those in need, such as the poor, sick, or elderly.	
5	I am comfortable leading a group or committee.	
6	I enjoy studying and teaching the Bible.	
7	I am known for having a positive and uplifting attitude.	
8	I feel a strong desire to spend time in prayer for others.	
9	I am skilled at identifying practical needs and finding ways to meet them.	
10	I have a talent for managing finances and resources wisely.	
11	I feel a strong passion for creating a welcoming and inclusive environment.	
12	I often feel prompted to help others grow in their faith.	
13	I enjoy working behind the scenes to ensure things run smoothly.	
14	I find joy in making things beautiful or creating art that inspires others.	

15	I am often moved to give generously to others in need or to support my church/community.	
16	I find it easy to understand and explain complex concepts.	
17	I feel a strong sense of responsibility to care for God's creation.	
18	I enjoy bringing people together and building a sense of community.	
19	I feel a special empathy for those who are hurting or in distress.	
20	I often feel compelled to speak out against injustice or to defend those who are oppressed.	

Scoring:

After you have completed the assessment, add up the scores for each statement. Higher scores in particular areas indicate a stronger presence of that spiritual gift.

Spiritual Gifts Summary:

Gift	**Statement Numbers**	**Total Score**
Administration	1, 5, 10	
Evangelism	2, 12, 18	
Encouragement	3, 7, 19	
Mercy	4, 8, 19	
Leadership	1, 5, 18	
Teaching	6, 16, 19	
Hospitality	11, 15, 18	
Serving	9, 13, 17	
Artistic Creativity	14, 17, 19	

Giving	15, 18, 20	
Knowledge/Wisdom	6, 16, 20	
Prophecy	8, 20, 12	

Reflection:

Based on your scores, identify your top 3 spiritual gifts. Reflect on how you can use these gifts to serve others and glorify God.

Top 3 Spiritual Gifts:

1. ______________________________

2. ______________________________

3. ______________________________

Action Plan:

Write down specific ways you can use your spiritual gifts in your church or community. Set goals for developing and using your spiritual gifts.

Using Your Gifts:

1. ______________________________

2. ______________________________

3. ______________________________

Goals:

1. ______________________________

2. ______________________________

3. ______________________________

Appendix C

Spiritual Vulnerabilities Assessment

Understanding one's spiritual vulnerabilities is crucial for growth and protection in faith. This assessment helps individuals identify areas where they may be susceptible to spiritual challenges, allowing them to take proactive steps to strengthen their spiritual resilience.

Spiritual Vulnerabilities Assessment

Read each statement and decide how well it describes you. Use the following scale to respond to each statement:

5 - Strongly Agree
4 - Agree
3 - Neutral
2 - Disagree
1 - Strongly Disagree

Write the number that corresponds to your response in the space provided.

Personal Information:

Name: ______________________________

Date: _______________________________

Assessment Statements:

#	Statement	Response (1-5)
1	I often feel overwhelmed by fear or anxiety.	
2	I struggle to trust God in difficult situations.	
3	I find it hard to forgive others who have hurt me.	
4	I frequently feel distant from God or spiritually dry.	
5	I am easily discouraged when faced with obstacles.	
6	I tend to isolate myself from others, especially during tough times.	
7	I struggle with feelings of anger or bitterness.	
8	I have difficulty maintaining a regular prayer life.	
9	I often feel tempted by things that lead me away from God.	
10	I find it hard to let go of worries about the future.	
11	I struggle with self-doubt and feelings of inadequacy.	
12	I often compare myself to others and feel inferior.	
13	I have trouble finding joy in my daily life.	
14	I feel guilty or ashamed about past mistakes and sins.	
15	I find it hard to trust in God's plan for my life.	
16	I struggle with negative thoughts and attitudes.	
17	I feel unworthy of God's love and grace.	
18	I find it hard to study and understand the Bible.	
19	I am easily influenced by negative or unholy influences.	
20	I have difficulty staying committed to my faith practices.	

Scoring:

After you have completed the assessment, add up the scores for each statement. Higher scores in particular areas indicate stronger vulnerabilities.

Spiritual Vulnerabilities Summary:

Vulnerability	Statement Numbers	Total Score
Fear and Anxiety	1, 5, 10	
Trust Issues	2, 15, 17	
Unforgiveness	3, 7, 14	
Spiritual Dryness	4, 8, 18	
Isolation	6, 12, 19	
Discouragement	5, 11, 16	
Temptation	9, 19, 20	
Negative Thoughts	16, 12, 11	

Reflection:

Based on your scores, identify your top 3 spiritual vulnerabilities. Reflect on how these vulnerabilities affect your spiritual life and relationships.

Top 3 Spiritual Vulnerabilities:

1. ____

2. ____

3. ____

Action Plan:

Write down specific steps you can take to address and overcome your spiritual vulnerabilities. Set goals for spiritual growth and resilience.

Steps to Overcome Vulnerabilities:

1. ____

2. ____

3. ____

Spiritual Growth Goals:

1. ____

2. ____

3. ____

Appendix D

Anger Assessment Template

This Anger Assessment is designed to help identify and understand anger patterns. By reflecting on your statements and recording your responses, you can gain insights into how anger affects your life and identify areas where you might need to seek support or make changes.

Assessment Instructions

Read each statement carefully. Rate your response on a scale of 1 to 5, where 1 means "Never" and 5 means "Always." Be honest with yourself for the most accurate assessment.

Anger Assessment Statements

#	**Statement**	**Response (1-5)**
1	I often feel irritated or annoyed over small issues.	
2	I find it difficult to control my temper when things don't go my way.	
3	I hold grudges against people who have wronged me.	
4	I frequently argue with family members, friends, or colleagues.	
5	I experience physical symptoms (like a racing heart or tense muscles) when I am angry.	
6	I tend to withdraw from others when I am angry.	

7	I feel guilty or ashamed after an angry outburst.	
8	I have been told by others that I have a problem with anger.	
9	I find it hard to forgive and forget when someone has upset me.	
10	I often think about past events that made me angry.	
11	I have damaged relationships because of my anger.	
12	I use substances (like alcohol or drugs) to manage my anger.	
13	I feel out of control when I get angry.	
14	I raise my voice or yell when I am angry.	
15	I have broken objects or thrown things when I am angry.	
16	I often regret things I said or did when I was angry.	
17	I find it hard to calm down quickly after getting angry.	
18	I feel that people often take advantage of me, making me angry.	
19	I have been involved in physical fights because of my anger.	
20	I struggle to find healthy ways to express my anger.	

Anger Assessment Summary

Anger Trigger	**Statement Numbers**	**Total Score**
Irritation and Annoyance	1, 4, 18	
Temper Control	2, 13, 17	
Grudges and Forgiveness	3, 9, 10	
Physical Symptoms	5, 6, 7	
Relationship Impact	8, 11, 19	

Substance Use	12, 15, 20	
Regret and Guilt	7, 16, 17	
Expression of Anger	14, 15, 20	

Scoring and Interpretation

1-20 Points: Low Anger Levels – Your anger seems to be well-managed. Continue practicing healthy coping strategies.

21-40 Points: Moderate Anger Levels – You might experience occasional issues with anger. Consider exploring more effective anger management techniques.

41-60 Points: High Anger Levels – Anger is a significant issue in your life. It is advisable to seek professional support or counseling.

61-80 Points: Severe Anger Levels – Your anger is likely affecting multiple areas of your life. Professional intervention is strongly recommended.

Appendix E

Pornographic Addiction Assessment

This Pornographic Addiction Assessment is designed to help identify and understand patterns and behaviors related to the consumption of pornographic material. By reflecting on your statements and recording your responses, you can gain insight into how pornography affects your life and identify areas where you might need to seek support or make changes.

Assessment Instructions

Read each statement carefully. Rate your response on a scale of 1 to 5, where 1 means "Never" and 5 means "Always." Be honest with yourself for the most accurate assessment.

Pornographic Addiction Assessment Statements

#	Statement	Response (1-5)
1	I think about watching pornography often, even when I am doing other activities.	
2	I feel unable to control my urge to watch pornography.	
3	Watching pornography interferes with my daily responsibilities (work, school, family).	
4	I feel ashamed or guilty after watching pornography.	

5	I use pornography to cope with stress or negative emotions.	
6	I have tried to stop watching pornography but have been unsuccessful.	
7	My consumption of pornography has increased over time.	
8	I prefer watching pornography over being intimate with my partner.	
9	I neglect important aspects of my life (relationships, hobbies) due to pornography use.	
10	I lie or hide my pornography use from others.	
11	I feel the need to watch more extreme or graphic content to achieve the same level of arousal.	
12	My use of pornography has caused conflicts in my relationships.	
13	I spend a significant amount of time planning or fantasizing about watching pornography.	
14	I feel anxious or restless if I am unable to watch pornography.	
15	I watch pornography in inappropriate places or situations.	
16	I use pornography despite it having negative consequences on my life.	
17	My pornography use affects my self-esteem or body image.	
18	I feel disconnected from reality due to my pornography use.	
19	I have lost interest in activities I once enjoyed because I prefer watching pornography.	
20	I engage in risky behaviors to access pornography.	

Pornographic Addiction Assessment Summary

Addiction Trigger	**Statement Numbers**	**Total Score**
Preoccupation	1, 13, 17	
Loss of Control	2, 6, 16	
Interference with Responsibilities	3, 9, 19	
Emotional Impact	4, 5, 14	
Escalation	7, 11, 20	
Relationship Impact	8, 12, 10	
Secrecy	10, 15, 18	

Scoring and Interpretation

1-20 Points: Low Addiction Levels – Your pornography use seems to be under control. Continue practicing healthy habits.

21-40 Points: Moderate Addiction Levels – You might experience occasional issues with pornography use. Consider exploring more effective coping strategies.

41-60 Points: High Addiction Levels – Pornography use is a significant issue in your life. It is advisable to seek professional support or counselling.

61-80 Points: Severe Addiction Levels – Your pornography use is likely affecting multiple areas of your life. Professional intervention is strongly recommended.

Appendix F

Sex Addiction Assessment

This Sex Addiction Assessment is designed to help identify and understand patterns and behaviors related to sexual activities. By reflecting on the statements and recording responses, you can gain insight into how these behaviors affect your life and identify areas where you might need to seek support or make changes.

Assessment Instructions

Read each statement carefully. Rate your response on a scale of 1 to 5, where 1 means "Never" and 5 means "Always." Be honest with yourself for the most accurate assessment.

Sex Addiction Assessment Statements

#	**Statement**	**Response (1-5)**
1	I often find myself preoccupied with sexual thoughts or fantasies.	
2	I feel unable to control my sexual urges or behaviors.	
3	My sexual behaviors interfere with my daily responsibilities (work, school, family).	
4	I feel ashamed or guilty after engaging in sexual activities.	

5	I use sex as a way to cope with stress or negative emotions.	
6	I have tried to reduce or stop my sexual activities but have been unsuccessful.	
7	My desire for sex has increased over time, requiring more frequent or intense activities.	
8	I prioritize sexual activities over being intimate in non-sexual ways with my partner.	
9	I neglect important aspects of my life (relationships, hobbies) due to my sexual behaviors.	
10	I lie or hide my sexual behaviors from others.	
11	I feel the need to engage in more extreme or risky sexual activities to achieve the same satisfaction.	
12	My sexual behaviors have caused conflicts in my relationships.	
13	I spend a significant amount of time planning or fantasizing about sexual activities.	
14	I feel anxious or restless if I am unable to engage in sexual activities.	
15	I engage in sexual activities in inappropriate places or situations.	
16	I continue to engage in sexual behaviors despite knowing they have negative consequences.	
17	My sexual behaviors affect my self-esteem or body image.	
18	I feel disconnected from reality due to my sexual activities.	
19	I have lost interest in activities I once enjoyed because I prefer engaging in sexual activities.	
20	I engage in illegal or dangerous behaviors to satisfy my sexual urges.	

Sex Addiction Assessment Summary

Addiction Trigger	**Statement Numbers**	**Total Score**
Preoccupation	1, 13, 17	
Loss of Control	2, 6, 16	
Interference with Responsibilities	3, 9, 19	
Emotional Impact	4, 5, 14	
Escalation	7, 11, 20	
Relationship Impact	8, 12, 10	
Secrecy	10, 15, 18	

Scoring and Interpretation

1-20 Points: Low Addiction Levels – Your sexual behaviors seem to be under control. Continue practicing healthy habits.

21-40 Points: Moderate Addiction Levels – You might experience occasional issues with sexual behaviors. Consider exploring more effective coping strategies.

41-60 Points: High Addiction Levels – Sexual behaviors are a significant issue in your life. It is advisable to seek professional support or counseling.

61-80 Points: Severe Addiction Levels – Your sexual behaviors are likely affecting multiple areas of your life. Professional intervention is strongly recommended.

Appendix G

Temperament Assessment

This Temperament Assessment is designed to help understand personality traits and how they influence your interactions and behavior. By reflecting on the statements and recording your responses, you can gain insight into your temperament and identify areas of personal growth.

Assessment Instructions

Read each statement carefully. Rate your response on a scale of 1 to 5, where 1 means "Never" and 5 means "Always." Be honest with yourself for the most accurate assessment.

Temperament Assessment Statements

#	Statement	Response (1-5)
1	I enjoy social gatherings and meeting new people.	
2	I prefer to plan my activities and stick to a schedule.	
3	I am quick to express my feelings and emotions.	
4	I find it easy to adapt to new situations and environments.	
5	I am often reflective and think deeply about my actions and decisions.	

6	I prefer a quiet and calm environment over a busy and noisy one.	
7	I tend to take charge and lead in group settings.	
8	I am sensitive to the feelings and needs of others.	
9	I enjoy taking risks and trying new things.	
10	I feel more comfortable following a routine rather than improvising.	
11	I often feel anxious or stressed in unfamiliar situations.	
12	I am patient and can wait for things without getting frustrated.	
13	I like to have clear goals and work systematically towards them.	
14	I am spontaneous and enjoy the freedom of making decisions on the go.	
15	I find it easy to forgive others and let go of grudges.	
16	I am detail-oriented and pay attention to small aspects of tasks.	
17	I often seek out exciting and stimulating experiences.	
18	I value stability and consistency in my life.	
19	I am empathetic and can easily understand others' emotions.	
20	I find it hard to stay focused on long-term projects.	

Temperament Assessment Summary

Temperament Dimension	Statement Numbers	Total Score
Extraversion	1, 4, 7, 9, 14, 17	
Introversion	2, 5, 6, 10, 12, 18	
Emotional Stability	3, 11, 15, 19	
Conscientiousness	8, 13, 16, 20	

Scoring and Interpretation

Extraversion vs. Introversion: High scores in Extraversion suggest a sociable and outgoing personality, while high scores in Introversion indicate a preference for solitude and introspection.

Emotional Stability: Higher scores suggest greater control over emotions and less susceptibility to stress and anxiety.

Conscientiousness: Higher scores indicate a methodical and organized approach to tasks, while lower scores suggest a more spontaneous and flexible attitude.

Total Score Ranges

Extraversion/Introversion:

6-18: Introverted tendencies

19-30: Balanced

31-36: Extraverted tendencies

Emotional Stability:

4-8: Low emotional stability

9-12: Moderate emotional stability

13-20: High emotional stability

Conscientiousness:

4-8: Low conscientiousness

9-12: Moderate conscientiousness

13-20: High conscientiousness

www.ingramcontent.com/pod-product-compliance
Lightning Source LLC
LaVergne TN
LVHW021153160826
845679LV00024B/2100

* 9 7 9 8 8 9 4 7 5 4 6 7 3 *